SPIRIT BY THE SEA TRILOGY
TRAVEL TO DESTINY - BOOK TWO

APRIL AUTRY

COPYRIGHT©2018 - GALACTIC GRANDMOTHER®

ALL RIGHTS RESERVED

No part of this book shall be reproduced or transmitted in any form or by any means without prior written permission of the publisher. No liability is assumed for damages resulting from the use of the information contained herein. This is a work of fiction. Names, characters, places and incidents either are the product of author's imagination or are used fictionally. Any resemblance to actual events or locales or persons, living or dead, is entirely coincidental.

https://GalacticGrandmother.com
https://info@galacticgrandmother.com

ALSO BY APRIL AUTRY

Galactic Grandmother Past Life Series

ATLANTIS, JOURNEY FROM THE INNER TEMPLE

MY LIFE WITH JESUS

ESCAPE FROM MALDEK

Galactic Grandmother Spiritual Journey Series

WORKING IN THE QUANTUM FIELD, BOOK 1 & 2

MULTIDIMENSIONAL ASPECTS - HIGHER SELVES

CHAPTER 1

"It is big!" the holy man said, looking at the new medicine basket I had on my shoulders.
"I made it to carry all my medicine." I told him.
"Yes." he nodded, and walked around to see it.
"Good," he said, "when will you return?"
"At the big moon."
The holy man smiled, "I like that you travel to the villages."
"I enjoy it." I said, "do you think of the mountain camp?"
"Yes," he said and smiled, "I do not think of sleeping on the trail."
I laughed, "You enjoy your hut!"
"And the food!" he laughed, and slapped his belly.

I TRAVEL around the island now, and he stays on the flat lands. He and Konani care for the villagers here. His brother's women keep his hut clean, and feed him well. Also Konani has children that call him "grandfather."

I looked at the holy man, and he looked older. He has lines on his face, and light hair mixed with his dark. He also walks slower, and sits at the fire pit more.

I am also older, I am a man, and I am strong. I stand as high as the holy man, and higher than Konani. My arms and legs are strong, from walking the island trails carrying heavy medicine baskets, and I still swim each day. When I am on the flat lands, I swim in the ocean, and when I am at the mountain camp, I swim in the river pools.

Now, when I enter a village, many young women bring me food and smile. Also, fathers, have asked me to join with their daughters, yet these young women are as sisters to me. My eyes never look upon them, as Konani looked at Leilani. I am happy traveling the island, from village to village. I also enjoy the peace of the mountain camp, and will go there for many moons to make medicines, and speak with the ancestors. I do not need a woman to care for me, and I would not be happy staying in a village to care for a family.

"Tell your father I spoke of him." the holy man said.

I nodded, my father no longer fished, and complained many times of hurting in his chest. He is a grandfather now. He spends his days sitting under the palm trees, weaving baskets, and talking with the other old men.

"Tell Konani I will bring back mountain tea."

"He will like that!"

He put his hand on my shoulder, and smiled, "Travel well".

I nodded, turned, and walked away feeling happy to travel again.

I DID NOT GO on the trail past Konani's house, and through the mountain to the other side of the island. I will travel along the sea, then up to the mountain village, with the sickness of their ancestors. I travel there, when I need more mud for medicine. It has been many moons, and I need it now. Also, my teacher has told me there is a boy I need to see.

I walk along the sand, and think of the day we saw Maleko on this trail. We did not know, that Maleko's oldest daughter, would join with Konani.

"We do not know, who will join us on our path," I thought, "or what will happen." I thought of the holy man coming into my village, and did not know, I would leave my family to learn medicine. I did not know the holy man, and Konani, would be my brothers in the circle of medicine men, yet the ancestors knew this.

"Thank you," I said, "for guiding me."

My teacher tells me many things, such as seeing a boy in the mountain village, yet when I ask her where I will meet my woman, she will not say.

"Walk your path." she says, and no more.

I learned to listen to my own voice. I also look for signs in my dreams, and in the visions that come into my head. I speak with Konani on many things, and the holy man gives me council as well.

I STAND ON THE SAND, looking up at the trail into the mountain. I see where it starts, yet it quickly goes under thick trees that hide it.

"I do not like this trail." I thought.

The air is hot, it is hard to breath, and I know the sickness is there. My heart hurts for the villagers that suffer this sickness, yet no medicines have helped. I give tea to help them sleep, or for sore bones, yet the sickness is stronger than my medicine. When I travel here, I wonder why the villagers stay. I move the basket on my shoulders, and take in a big breath of cool air.

"Protect me," I spoke to my teacher, "and guide me to the boy."

I walk across the sand, and start climbing the cliff, up to the mountain trail. I did not want to go, yet I told myself, "I am blessed, let me help the villagers that are not."

I still felt the sea wind, on the back of my arms and legs, as I walked into the trees. The trail quickly went up, and was hard, yet my strong legs and back carried the heavy basket. I breathed in deep, and smiled to myself. I thought of the boy I had been, how hard it was to carry my own bed roll, and walk on the trails behind the holy man. I was happy with my man's body. I did not have a belly like Konani, or the holy man. I looked down, it was flat, and hard. I stood straight, and higher than most men, and I smiled much. I was glad that I learned how to make medicine, and that I helped the villagers.

The ancestors had known this would make me happy, and that I would be a good medicine man. I thought of the holy man asking me if I was happy, and if I wanted to be his assistant. As a boy, I had not thought of this, yet I knew I wanted to go.

Then I knew why I thought of this. "The boy will be a new assistant!"

"Yes."

I laughed, "You guided my thoughts!"

I have learned that my teacher, many times, guides my thoughts. I learned to see this, and now know, how closely our teachers are with us.

I WALKED WITH BIG STEPS, I needed to gather mud for medicine, and I wanted to see this boy. I smelled the bubbling pool of water before I saw it. Many plants had grown up to hide the water. I walked off the trail, followed the smell, and pushed away the high plants. Warm water bubbled up from the pond, and it was not the color of sea water or river water. This water looked like the sky, after the sun has gone down. It was the color of flowers, yet the smell was not of flowers. I squatted down and scooped it into my hand, then squeezed the water out, making a ball of mud. I made many balls, and lay them on the ground next to me. When finished, I gathered leaves to wrap the mud balls, before putting them in my basket. I pushed them down into the bottom of my basket, knowing they would drip, and I did not want my other medicines to get wet.

"Good," I thought, "I am ready to see the new assistant."

I put the basket on my shoulders, and turned quickly to walk back on the trail. I wondered if the boy would be young, and if I would carry his basket, as the holy man had done for me. I thought of the sickness in the village, then wondered if he would be sick.

"He is not sick." my teacher said.

I have talked more to my teacher since traveling by myself, and I sing many songs from my old village, songs my mother sang to me as a boy. I also listen to the birds, and sing to them. My belly made noise, and I grabbed dried fish from my basket, then fresh fruit from a tree near the trail. These fruit, had the sweet juice the holy man liked. I picked many, drinking the juice, and putting others in my basket.

I thought how I had waited to look at what the holy man carried for ceremonies. "I will look for a boy such as I was."

"He will ask me about being a medicine man." I thought, "as I asked Konani.

I felt the mud balls dripping on my leg, and stopped, to pack more leaves around them.

"I will teach him as Konani taught me," I thought, "and he will think I am a good teacher."

I swung the basket back on, and was glad that I would have a helper.

"He will make the tea, and clean!" I thought, and laughed.

AFTER WALKING UNDER THE TREES, the village clearing opened-up, with bright sun shining down. I heard sounds of the village, with women working, and children playing. The older village men sat around the fire pit talking, and weaving baskets. The village looked like any other, then I came closer, and saw them. A little boy chased other boys, trying to run on feet, that were eaten away from the sickness. An old man held a basket, with a hand that looked like the claw of a large shell. A young mother's face, was marked with open wounds, as she sat feeding her baby. I wondered again, why this sickness had come to the village, and asked my teacher.

"You cannot know this." she said.

I have learned, that she would tell me when I was ready, or when I needed to know.

I walked to the men sitting around the fire pit.

"Welcome." an old man said.

"Sit." another told me.

I took my basket off, and sat down.

"How is your village?" I asked, and drank water from my pouch.

"We are the same." An old man said, and the others nodded.

"We eat, we sleep, and watch the village!" he said.

The men laughed, and I laughed with them.

"I have medicine, tell me who needs it."

The men nodded, and began to talk of many villagers.

I stood, and grabbed my basket.

The man with the claw hand stood up, "I will take you to my daughter."

"She is bad." another said.

THE MAN WALKED with stiff legs. They did not bend, and when he stepped, he leaned to each side. I followed him, and was glad that I walked with smooth steps, placing one foot ahead of the other.

He stopped at the doorway of a hut, "Do you sleep?" he called inside.

"No father." a woman's voice called back.

A boy walked to the doorway, and smiled at the old man. "Grandfather!"

We stepped into the hut, and I saw the woman on her mat.

"Welcome." she said.

I smiled and went to her. "How are you?" I asked, and saw her face was hot.

"I cannot leave my mat."

The boy came to stand by me.

"Do you eat?"

"No." she said, looking at me, then to her son.

"I give her fruit," the boy said, "it does not stay in her belly."

I reached down, and felt the hot skin on her face.

"She needs cold water. She needs to drink it, and be washed with it."

"I will get it." the boy said, and left.

The old man held her hand, and looked at her. "Her mother, and her man have passed."

She looked in my eyes, "I will pass soon."

I saw water come into her father's eyes.

"My son does not have the sickness," she told me, "I want him to leave the village."

I looked at her, and wondered if this was the boy, that would be the new assistant.

"Why do you say this?"

"My man passed when he was young, I raised up my son..." she said, and stopped.

I felt the hurt in her heart, she looked at her father, then back at me.

"I want him to find a woman in another village."

I nodded, she wanted her son to join with a woman, that did not have the sickness.

"After I pass," she said, "I want my son to leave."

"I will take him" her father told her.

She looked at me, then to him, "You are too old to travel."

I knew that she wanted me, to take her son away from this village.

"Is this the boy?" I thought.

"Yes" came quickly into my head.

I had not looked into the boy's eyes, to know he wanted this. I had not spoken to the holy man of a new assistant, and did not know, if he wanted me to bring him back. I just started to travel around the island, and was not ready to care for the boy.

"I need to travel to other villages," I said looking at her, "I will return on my way back."

She did not speak, her eyes still looked into mine. I knew she waited for me, to say I would take him.

"I will talk to your son of leaving, when I come back."

She smiled, and water came into her eyes. "Thank you." she said, "where do you live?"

"I live by the sea, on flat land, where there are many villages."

"Good." she said.

"He will learn to fish." I told her.

"He does not like to fish."

"I did not like to fish," I said, "I learned medicine."

"Will you teach him?" she asked.

"Yes." I heard my teacher say.

"I will teach him."

She nodded, and her father smiled, "This is good"

THE BOY WALKED BACK into the hut, carrying a pot of water from the stream. He dipped a cup from it, and held his mother's head up, to sip the water.

"What is your name?" I asked.

"Laka" he said, and gently put his mother's head back down.

"Do you want to learn medicine?"

He looked at me, "Medicine?"

"I will teach you to make medicine."

He looked at his mother, then at me. I saw he was small and boney, yet not as young as I thought.

"He cared for his mother," my teacher whispered, "not for himself."

"I want you to leave after I pass." his mother said.

The boy looked at her, then his grandfather, "Where will I go?"

"I will take you to my village." I told him.

His mouth hung open, and he did not speak.

"The holy man that taught me medicine lives there, and another medicine man."

"I will not leave my mother."

"After I pass," she looked at him, "you will go."

He shook his head, "We will not speak of this now."

I nodded to the mother, "I will come back."

I bent down, and grabbed a pouch, with strong medicine from my basket.

"Give her cool water all day, wash her with it at night, then make this tea."

The boy took the pouch, and looked inside.

"It is strong, use this much." I said, and put leaves between my fingers, "she will sleep well."

"Thank you." she said, and held out her hand to me.

I took her hand, squeezed it, and saw a vision in my head. Her son was an old man, smiling.

I smiled at her, "Your son will be a happy old man."

Water ran down her cheeks, she nodded, "This is what I want."

She looked at her son, "Laka, when he returns, I want you to leave."

He looked at her, yet did not speak.

"This is what I want." she told him.

He nodded, and I saw water in his eyes.

"We will speak when I return." I said, then picked up my basket, "I will give medicine to the others."

I walked out of the hut, and stood looking across the village.

"You guided me to him," I thought, "as the holy man was guided to me."

I thought of traveling with this boy back to see the holy man.

"I wonder if the holy man knows of the boy, and did not tell me."

Like my teacher, the holy man did not tell me all he knew. He let me walk my path, and find my own way. I wanted to see this boy, yet I did not know if I was ready, to teach and care for a new assistant. I thought of taking him to the medicine man's camp, yet the holy man did not travel there now.

"He will stay on the flat lands with the holy man," I thought, "when he is older, I will take him to the medicine man's camp."

I LEFT the village when the sun was low, and walked fast. The many trees and bushes by the trail did not let the air blow, and I was hot. Water rolled down my face, and I walked faster. When my belly was hungry, I grabbed dried fish from my pack, yet did not stop. I picked fruit from the trees that I passed, and drank much water from my pouch. I took long steps, and felt my strong legs under me.

"I will run!" I thought, and held my basket on each side, as I ran down the trail.

I started fast, then slowed down as the sun stopped shining through the trees.

My body was wet from running, and darkness was falling. I

stopped and looked around, I saw an area under a tree where no bushes grew, and walked there. I spread out my bedroll, grabbed my pouch for a drink, then used the water to wash my face. I lay down on my side, and felt my legs sticking together.

"I will swim in the waves soon." I thought, and closed my eyes to sleep.

I AWOKE, and pushed my hair back. My face and neck were wet again, and I reached in the basket for a string to tie my hair back. I looked at my arms and legs, I was covered with dirt from the trail, and shook my head.

"This mountain!"

CHAPTER 2

As I walked, my thoughts returned to the boy. His life was hard. His father passed when he was young, he had cared for his mother, and now she would pass. When my mother passed, leaving with the holy man, helped my heart to heal. I traveled to new villages, and learned to make medicine. The holy man made me swim, and carry heavy baskets, so I grew strong.

"He needs to grow strong." I thought.

A SEA BIRD cried loudly over my head. I took in a big breath of air, and smiled to myself.

"I am close!"

I walked faster, and looked ahead, to see the sea through the trees. I would reach my father's village this day, and feast on fish that my brothers caught. I reached the cliff above the sand, and climbed down. I took off my basket, and ran into the water.

"Thank you Mother!" I cried out, and dove under a wave, feeling my body washed by it.

I swam with the waves, and enjoyed myself. Laying on a rock to dry, I looked at the water, and thought of when Konani said it gives us much. It gives us fish, shells, sea plants to eat, and to use for medicine.

"I enjoy watching the water." I thought, and looked past the waves.

Suddenly I saw water spraying high into the air, then another, and I knew these were the big fish that my brothers spoke of. The large dark fish with wide tails, that came up to blow water into the sky. I stood, and watched the sprays get smaller, as the fish swam away. Then I looked down, at the water splashing against the rocks, and saw black shells growing under the water.

"I will bring these to my family." I thought, and went back to my basket to get my blade. I took the sharp blade out of a pouch, and climbed back on the rocks. I laid down on my belly, and stretched my arm down into the water. I cut a shell from the rock, and held it up, to look at. The shell was closed, and shined with the water.

"Good!"

I was gathering more shells, when I heard voices. I stopped and lay quiet.

"Where are they?"

I looked up the mountain trail, then on the sand, along the water. Again, I heard voices.

"Is that singing?" I thought.

The voices sounded louder, and came from behind me. I sat up to look carefully across the water.

"There!" I shouted. Jumping to my feet, I saw boats traveling toward my father's village.

They were far out on the water, and looked small, yet I knew these were not fisherman. There were many in each boat, paddling together, pushing the boat fast along the water. My heart pounded, I wondered who they were. I quickly gathered up the shells into my arms, and ran back across the rocks. I pulled out pouches of medicines, throwing them on the sand, and stuffed the shells down on top of the mud balls. Then threw the pouches in the basket, and slung it on my shoulders.

"Is it Kekoa?" I wondered, then, "warriors from another island?"

I ran down the beach, and my basket bounced up and down. I ran along the hard sand, and looked ahead, so that I did not step on sharp shells.

"I want to fly like a bird!"

As I RAN, I watched the boats travel far ahead of me. I dug my feet into the sand and ran faster, wondering if the travelers would stop at my father's village. I reached the high rocks that protected the village, and climbed quickly to the top. I looked down, and did not see the traveler's boats.

"They went past!" I thought, "They return to the grandfather's village!"

I was happy, as I climbed down, and walked on the sand. I looked toward the village, saw many men standing at the fire pit, and I started to run again.

"Kai!" Jatu called out, and came to me, "it is good you are back!"

"Father!" I said, and walked to him, placing a hand on his shoulder, "Did you see the boats pass?"

"Yes! They travel fast!"

"I think they travel to the grandfather's village." I told them.

My father nodded, "The young have returned."

There was much talk about the travelers, and laughter. The men spoke of taking their boats to the grandfather's village.

"I will go with you." I said.

"We will leave when the sun rises." Jatu told me.

I gave him the shells from my basket, and my brother put them by the fire.

The villagers gathered around the fire pit, and spoke of the travelers. My brother's woman walked to me, carrying a child on her hip.

"He is big!" I said.

She smiled, "He looks like his father."

I was glad to see my family, and wondered if I would return here when I was old, as the holy man had returned to his family. We ate much fish, the shells, and fruit. My belly was full when I stood.

"Great Mother," I called out, and the villagers got quiet, "Thank you for filling our bellies."

The villagers nodded their heads.

"Ancestors, guide us to fish and protect the village."

"Yes!" Jatu yelled, and the others joined in.

"I have medicine," I told them, "come to me."

I sat, and looked at my father. He smiled at me, I knew he was glad that I learned medicine, and now spoke to the ancestors.

I gave medicine to the villagers, then stood. "I will sleep."

I thought of the holy man saying this, as I walked from the fire pit.

I PUT my bedroll on the high sand, looking over the water. The moon was not big, yet the light shined down, and sparkled on the water. The air was warm, and a gentle wind blew to me, from the waves. Villagers had gone to their huts, the fire pit was quiet, and I enjoyed the sounds of the waves. I lay down, and put my hands behind my head. I thought of the boats that passed quickly on the water.

"Those were not fishing boats," I thought, "they were built to travel."

"I wonder where their island is." I lay there looking at the lights in the sky, thinking of the travelers, and my eyes grew tired. I closed them, and soon slept.

"GET UP!" Jatu shouted, "eat." He bent down, and put a palm leaf on my belly, with hot fish and fruit on it.

I rubbed my eyes, and held the palm leaf, as I sat up. The fish smelled good, and I grabbed some with my fingers, and put it into my mouth. I looked down the sand, where my brothers and others, put nets into the boats. I stuffed my mouth with the fish, and ate quickly. After finishing the fruit, and drinking water from my pouch, I stood up. I put my basket on, and ran to the boats. My father stood watching, and I went to him.

"Travel well." he said.

I helped push the boat into the water, then jumped in. I had not been in a boat since fishing with my father as a boy, and I was glad to be with my brothers, as we paddled out through the waves.

I dug my paddle into the water, and pulled it back, staying with my brothers paddles. Then we switched sides, again pushing the paddle down, and pulling it back. My brothers led the paddling, with strokes on each side, of the small fishing boat. I thought of the long boats I saw with the travelers, and many paddled. I knew how they could glide through the water, so smoothly and quickly.

We were paddling well, yet not as fast. We paddled through the waves, and on the other side, the boat went up and down. We came to where the sea plants grow, and many fish and sea birds eat. I looked back to the sand, and saw villagers still watching us.

"Are you stopping to fish?" Jatu called out to men, as we passed their boat. We laughed, and the men paddled faster to catch us. I felt my arms and shoulders working, and was glad that swimming had made me strong.

"You paddle well." my brother called from behind.

"I have not been in a boat since I was young." I said, and laughed.

"Fish with us!" Jatu said.

I laughed, "No, I am not a fisherman!"

My brothers also laughed, and we enjoyed being on the boat.

We traveled toward the grandfather's village. I watched the large sea birds fly above the waves, and dive down, to catch a fish in it's mouth. Then it sat on the water to eat. I also saw large fish swimming together, with great speed they jumped out of the water, and dove back in.

The sun was high above us now, and we had not stopped. We drank water, then paddled more. We did not let the boat slow, and the other men stayed behind us. We sang old songs from when we were boys, and talked of growing together in the village.

"You hid in the trees!" Jatu said.

"You stopped fishing with us!"

"I did not like to fish." I told them.

"You helped mother, and we helped father." Jatu said.

I nodded, and felt my heart hurt. I thought of mother, and saw myself as a young boy with her.

"I am glad I saw her before she passed." I told them.

"She passed young, like her sister." my brother said.

"We will see her again." I told them.

We got quiet, and each thought of mother, as we traveled.

"Look!" Jatu pointed ahead.

I saw the curve of sand, with boats resting there.

"The grandfather's village!" I yelled.

My heart pounded, when I saw a long boat resting, next to the smaller fishing boats.

"Not all the long boats are here." I said.

We turned the boat, and headed in with the waves. The waves pushed us, we rode in to where we could jump out, and pulled the boat up on the sand. I stood with my brothers, and the men from the other boat, looking at the long boats. We walked beside them, and looked at the long paddles.

"What kind of tree makes such a boat?" my brother asked.

"Welcome!" Men yelled, and walked to us from the fire pit. We walked back with them to the fire pit, where many villagers sat. I had not seen young men in this village, since they left with Kekoa.

"Do you travel with Kekoa?"

"Yes, we have returned to our elders' village." a young man answered, and an old man put his hand on the younger man's shoulder.

"I am glad I lived to see them return." the old man said.

"How is the new island?" I asked.

"It is good." he answered, "Kekoa led us to an island with good fishing, and many fruit trees."

"Where is he?"

"He went to his old village.

"I will be glad to see him." I said.

WE SAT around the fire pit, and listened to the young men. They told us of their return across the water, and how they did not stop paddling.

"We paddled at night, while others slept." they said, "when they woke, we slept."

"When you left," I said, "you traveled in small fishing boats with women and children."

The young men nodded, "We were those children."

"How long did you travel to see the new island?"

"I do not know," one said, "I was sick, and my mother held me."

"Travel was slow." another said.

"How did you find the new island?" I asked.

"We followed this island, after we passed it and went into the sea, we watched where the sea birds flew. At night, Kekoa showed us the stars to follow."

I nodded. I would not want to do this, I thought it was not safe. Yet Kekoa traveled on the sea here, to the new island, and now back.

"Will you return to your new village?" I asked.

"We will take the elders back in our boats, and lead others in fishing boats."

I looked around at the grandfathers, and grandmothers.

"Ancestors protect them." I thought.

THE YOUNG MEN told us of their new village, and the new island. We heard of babies coming in, and of huts that were built for the grandfathers and grandmothers.

"I am ready to travel!" a grandfather cried out.

"Yes," an old man said, "we will go." and he put his arm around his woman's shoulder. She smiled, yet her eyes held fear.

"When will you leave?" I asked.

"We will rest, and prepare to travel." a young man said, "Kekoa will tell us when to leave."

"Do you want to see the new village?" I asked Jatu.

"Yes," he said, "I want to see the new island, yet my family is here."

"We are fathers," my other brother said, "You go!"

I shook my head.

"No," I told him, "I like this island."

"No!" I thought to myself, "I do not want to travel on the sea!" I stood up, and my brothers looked at me.

"Do you want to swim?" I asked.

They shook their heads, and I walked down to the water.

I stood, and looked across the water, to where the sky and sea came together.

"I feel that I am fighting to stay here." I thought.

I ran into the water, a wave rushed to me, and I dove under. I came up on the other side, looked ahead, and saw another wave coming. I turned around to face the shore, and when the wave was at my back, I rose to the top, kicked my feet. I swam with the water, as it crashed down. I enjoyed playing in the water, and did not think of traveling to a new island. I swam out past the waves, and lay on my back in the water.

The sun was low, I knew I must get out of the water, and I looked for a big wave to swim in with. As I swam in, I leaned my head back in the water, then stood up. My wet hair fell down my back, and I shook my head, to shake the water out. I saw the men on the sand, point to the water behind me, and I turned to see a long boat coming. I walked out of the water, and waited on the sand. I wanted to see Kekoa, and smiled as they got closer.

THE LONG BOAT glided through the water, with men paddling on each side. The boat now turned toward the sand, and rode with a wave toward me. I saw the big shoulders of Kekoa, and waved to him. I watched as the men in front jumped out, to pull the boat in, then I saw a woman.

She sat holding a paddle, and when she stepped out of the boat, her long dark hair fell down to her waist. She had strong arms. She held the paddle, and pulled the boat in with the men. She wore a cloth, tied behind her neck, that hung down to where her long, strong legs started. I had not seen a woman such as this. Her skin was dark from the sun, she had dark markings on her arm and leg, such as Kekoa had.

"Kai!" Kekoa shouted.

He laughed and walked to me, yet I looked past him at the woman.

"You see my warrior woman!"

I looked at him, then back to the woman, "Who is she?"

"Her name is Milana."

"Milana! She is from this village!"

"You know her?" Kekoa asked.

"Yes, she was a girl when she left."

We watched her leave the boat, and run to an old man, sitting by the fire pit.

"Her grandfather." I said.

Kekoa nodded, "He is too old to travel."

CHAPTER 3

Kekoa had much to tell. He spoke of guiding the young people to the new island.

"We saw this island when I came here," he said, "There were no villages, so we did not stop."

"We have built a new village." he said, "and made a large fire pit."

"We built good huts." a young man said, "many more can be built."

"Are there other villages?" I asked.

"On the other side of the island." Kekoa said, "my son joined with a woman from there."

"I will also!" a young man said, and smiled, "she waits for me."

"This is good," I said, "is there a medicine man?"

"I have not seen a medicine man."

"Where are the other villagers from?" I asked.

"They left my island during the big battle."

"You did not know them?"

"No, these families where not from my village." Kekoa said.

"I have trained the young to be warriors, so they can protect the village, when I am too old."

Many young men laughed, "He is old now!" and Kekoa joined in the laughter.

. . .

I LISTENED to Kekoa and the young men talk of training, and I watched Milana. She sat on the other side of the fire pit, close to her grandfather, and spoke quietly to him. She put her lips on his cheek, and rubbed his arm. He smiled, and did not take his eyes from her.

"The little girl has grown." I thought. "She is a woman now."

I looked at the dark marking around her arm, it looked like the markings Kekoa had on his body. I looked around at the young men, and saw they also had dark markings on their skin.

"Why do you mark your bodies?" I asked Kekoa.

"Those are the marks of a warrior." he said.

"I did not know that women are warriors"

"There is no other woman warrior," he said, and looked at me. "She trained like a man, and fights like one also."

"Why?"

"She was angry to leave her grandfather. She said no man will tell her to leave again, and she learned to fight."

"That is the girl I knew!" I told him.

Yet, I looked at her now, and she was a gentle woman with her grandfather.

WE HAD a large fire in the pit, and a feast. We ate, and laughed much.

"Kai, say a blessing." Kekoa said.

The villagers got quiet, and looked to me. I stood, and put my arms up.

"We thank you Father for this day, we thank you Mother for the fish we feast on."

I dropped my arms, and closed my eyes. I took in a deep breath, blew it out, and opened my eyes. I looked around at the villagers, and saw Milana watching me.

"Ancestors, we thank you for guiding the young back to this village."

"Yes!" an old man called out, "thank you for bringing back our grandchildren."

Many people called out "thank you" to the ancestors, I looked into the darkness, beyond the fire pit, and saw the ancestors were here.

"We ask for your guidance, and for your protection." I looked around at the villagers, and they were happy. "Speak to your ancestors now."

I sat down, and watched them begin to talk with their families that had passed.

Kekoa leaned to me, "How is the holy man?"

"He is good. He does not travel now."

"Where is Konani?"

"He lives on the flat lands by the holy man. He has a woman and children!"

Kekoa leaned his head back, and laughed loud. "Konani is a father!" he shouted, and laughed more.

"The chief's son passed?"

I nodded my head, "Yes." then I told him of the battle.

We talked of many things, and as the fire burned lower, the villagers returned to their huts.

Kekoa stood up, "I will sleep."

I stood up also, "I will also."

Kekoa put his hand on my shoulder, "You have grown into a man. Do you have a woman?"

I shook my head, "No."

He smiled, "Milana has not joined with a man."

I shook my head, "Kekoa! Yet I was happy to hear this.

I WALKED TO THE SAND, where my brothers slept on their bed rolls. They made loud noises when they breathed, so I grabbed my bedroll, and walked away. I looked up at the moon, and did not look where I walked.

"Ouch!"

I looked down to see Milana.

"You stepped on me again!" She said.
"Are you hurt?"
"No!" she said, "the soft foot of a holy man cannot hurt me!"
I started to laugh.
"Why do you laugh?" She asked.
"You are the same Milana!"
"You are the same!" she said, "Stepping on me!"

I dropped my bed roll, and sat down. She sat with her legs crossed, looking at me, and her dark hair touched the sand.

"I am glad you came back for your grandfather." I told her.

She pushed her hair behind her shoulders, "I built a big hut for us."
"Are you happy there?"
"No! My grandfather is not there!"
She looked at the sea, "He wants me to go back with the others."
"He is old," I told her, "traveling would be hard for him."
"I know this!" she said, and shook her head.
I felt my teacher, and knew she would speak.
"She can learn medicine." my teacher said.
"When you were young," I said, "you wanted to learn medicine."
She looked at me, "Yes."
"Stay here with your grandfather," I told her, "I will teach you."
She was quiet, then spoke, "I will think on this."

She looked back at the water, and I watched her. She was not like the village girls, and I wanted to know more of her.

"Thank you Kai." She said, without looking at me.
"You know my name?" I asked.
"You know my name." She said.
"I thought many times of that little girl I stepped on!"

She hit me on the arm so quickly, that I did not see her hand coming.

"Ouch!" I called out, yet it did not hurt.
"That is for stepping on me then, and now!"
She stood, and looked down at me. "I go to my grandfather's hut."
I watched her walk away, "Sleep well."

. . .

I awoke with sand on my face. While I slept, I had rolled off my bedroll, and the side of my face was covered in sand. I sat up, and sand was also in my hair.

"I will swim." I thought, and ran down to the water and dived in. The water felt good. I looked back and saw my brothers eating by the fire pit, so I ran back to my bedroll, and leaned over to roll it up.

"You like to swim."

I turned around to see Milana, who looked at my wet body.

"Yes." I said, and looked down at her. Her eyes were dark, and I enjoyed looking into them.

"I have spoken to grandfather," she said, "I will stay with him, and learn medicine."

"Good."

She smiled, and looked into my eyes, "Good." Then she turned, and walked away.

I watched her, and saw the dark mark around her leg.

"Milana is a warrior," I thought, "and now she will learn medicine." I shook my head, "There is no other woman such as Milana!"

Then I thought of the holy man, "I wonder what the holy man will say, when I bring back new assistants!"

"We will fish on our way back." Jatu said, "Come with us."

I sat eating, and did not want to go. I wanted to stay and see Milana.

"Go," Kekoa said, "we have much to prepare."

I looked at him, "You will not leave?"

He laughed loudly, "I will wait for you to return!"

In my father's village, I had not gone to all the huts to give medicine. The villagers at the fire pit got medicine, yet I did not know if others lay in their huts.

"I will go." I told them, "and give more medicine in the village."

My brother slapped me on the back, "Finish eating!"

. . .

WE PUSHED the boat into the water, I jumped in, and grabbed a paddle. We worked together, taking the boat through the waves, then paddled hard to get away from the rocks. As we moved past them, I looked back over my shoulder. I saw many villagers, yet did not see Milana.

"What is this?" I thought, "I have not wanted to see other women, yet I want to see her."

We threw nets out, and pulled them behind the boat, as we paddled back to the village.

"It is good to fish with you Kai." my brother said, "Stay in the village with us."

I thought of staying in their village, and fishing each day. I wondered if I would have a family, then suddenly saw Milana's face, and thought she would be a good mother.

"Pull in the net!" Jatu shouted.

We put down our paddles, and started pulling it toward us. I saw fish jumping, as the net came up out of the water, and many were caught. We put the net in the boat, near our feet, and the fish still jumped in it.

"Good!" my other brother said, and we started to paddle again. Soon we saw the village, and I was glad to be back.

My father and others welcomed us, and helped carry the net full of fish, out of the boat. Women came to the net, and gathered fish, then took them back to prepare.

"Tell us of the travelers." my father said, and we walked to the fire pit, where the villagers waited to hear of the travelers from another island. We sat, talked, and ate.

My belly was full, and the sun was getting close to the water.

I stood up, "I will go to the huts, and give medicine."

I walked away, as my brothers still talked of the grandfather's village, and the young that had returned.

I gave many leaves to the old men and women, to make tea for their sore bones, and a mud ball to a new mother. I saw all the villagers that wanted medicine, and was happy they did not have bad wounds and sickness.

"I will leave when the sun comes up."

I stood back at the fire pit, and listened to the villagers. I enjoyed watching them, yet I was ready to sleep. I put my hand on father's shoulder.

"I will leave, and travel to the grandfather's village."

He turned his head to look at me, "Travel well."

I AWOKE when a drop of water fell on my face, then another, and the sun was hidden behind dark clouds. I heard a child crying, yet did not see villagers by the fire pit. I quickly rolled up my bedroll, grabbed my medicine bag, and ran to my brother's hut.

"Welcome! he said, as I came in.

I sat and ate with Jatu and his family.

"I need a fishing blanket to travel." I told him.

"I will not use it." he said. "We have much fish, and water will fall."

Jatu waited for me, to put my medicine basket on, then pulled the fishing blanket over my head.

"You will be dry." he said.

I put my hand on his shoulder, "Thank you brother."

I walked out of the village, and to the trail, that would take me to the grandfather's village. Water came down from the clouds, and I walked quickly. Soon the trail traveled higher, and wound around the mountain, that went out into the sea. I took my sandals off, and walked carefully on the muddy trail.

I thought how slowly I traveled when the holy man and Konani took me from my village. We had to sleep by the trail, and travel to the grandfather's village, when the sun rose again. Now I walked with long steps, not stopping to rest, and would reach the village when the sun went into the water. I wondered how fast the boy from the mountain village would travel, and thought he would be slow, as I had been.

"Milana has strong legs," I thought, "she will travel well."

The dark clouds with water, blew past, yet other clouds hid the sun. I did not know if more water would fall, and I kept walking with the fishing blanket on. Cool air blew, yet I was warm.

I was glad to return to the grandfathers' village. I wanted to see

Kekoa, and Milana. I watched the sun travel, and when it got close to the water, I knew I would soon come to the village. I thought of Konani. When he saw Leilani, and talked with her, he knew he wanted to join with her. I thought of my feelings for Milana.

"Will I want to join with her?" I thought, "yet I will be her teacher."

I knew I must think of her as a new assistant, as Laka will be.

"Help me be a good teacher."

CHAPTER 4

I was glad that I had not taken off the fishing blanket, more dark clouds poured water down before I reached the grandfather's village. I now stood above, looking at palm trees and huts, as the sun touched the water. I walked down the trail into the village, looking ahead to see Milana.

"Welcome!" Kekoa shouted from the fire pit, and walked to me. The other men stood, to see who was coming down the trail, so I waved at them.

"Your basket is heavy." he said.

"I brought much medicine."

"Let me see." he said, and walked around to my back. He pulled the wet fishing blanket off my head, then took the basket from my back.

"It is heavy." he said, as he lifted it with one hand, and moved it up and down.

"You are the strongest man I know!" I laughed, as I watched his big, strong arm.

He carried my basket, and I carried the fishing blanket, to the fire pit. The fire felt good, and warmed me.

"When will you see the holy man?" Kekoa asked.

"I go back soon. I must get a boy from the mountain village, who will be a new assistant."

Kekoa raised his eyebrows, "Milana will also learn medicine?"

"Yes."

"This is good," Kekoa nodded his head, "we need medicine in the new village."

"She will stay with her grandfather while she learns." I told him.

"She will not leave until he passes." Kekoa said.

"I want to see the holy man," Kekoa said, "I will travel with you."

"Good" I smiled, and was happy to hear this, "he will be happy to see you!"

When the sun rose, I went to see the villagers.

"How are you?" I stood in the doorway of a hut.

"Come in." an old man said.

I walked in, and saw Milana's grandfather, who sat on a cut log.

"Welcome." he said.

"Do you need medicine?"

"My old bones hurt, they wake me at night."

"I will give you leaves to make tea before bed, after that, put the wet hot leaves on your bones." I reached into my basket to find the leaves.

"Milana told me you will teach her medicine."

"Yes." I said, and handed him the pouch of leaves.

"She has wanted this since she was young."

"I know."

He looked at me, not knowing of what I spoke.

"I met her, after the holy man took me as a new assistant." I smiled, "and she wanted to know how she could learn."

He smiled, "She will be a good assistant."

" I looked around, "where is she?"

"She washes clothes."

"Is that all you need?" I asked.

He looked at me, and waved me to come closer. I leaned down to him, and he spoke quietly.

"When I pass, I want you to protect her."

I smiled, "She can protect herself."

He shook his head, "She is a woman," he looked into my eyes, "you are a man."

I looked at him, yet did not speak.

He grabbed my arm, "Join with her."

"I will protect her," I said quietly, "the ancestors will guide our joining."

He smiled broadly, "I can pass now, and know my granddaughter will be protected."

"What do you say?" Milana called from the door.

Her grandfather laughed, "Kai will teach you medicine, and protect you."

I grabbed my basket, and walked to her.

"I will protect myself!" she said, not smiling.

I smiled, and looked into her eyes, "I have given your grandfather medicine for his sore bones, and to help him sleep."

She looked at him, he held up the pouch. "Good." she said, and walked to him, not looking back at me.

I waved at him, and left.

I saw other villagers, sat with them and listened, and gave them medicines. Many elders needed the healing of talk and laughter. I began to know why the holy man used assistants to give out medicines. He talked much at the fire pits with men, helping guide the village, with what they must do. He gave blessings, called on the ancestors, and spoke for the ancestors when needed. He was able to do this, knowing his assistants gave out the medicines.

I RETURNED TO THE SAND, where Kekoa stood, watching his young warriors. The sounds of sticks hitting with great speed, and fierceness, made me look carefully at what they did.

"After this you will run!" Kekoa yelled.

"They train?" I asked.

He nodded, "They must train, and stay strong."

"Is the new village not safe?"

"Warriors can cross the sea." he said, and looked closely at the young men.

"Do you have others to fight?"

"I have trained young men from the other villages, we will join to protect our island."

I nodded, not wanting Milana to fight in such a battle, and knew why her grandfather wanted me to protect her.

"I will learn to fight." I told him.

Kekoa looked at me, "I will teach you, and Milana also." he said, and laughed loudly.

"She is a woman!"

"She is a warrior," Kekoa said, and yelled out, "put your sticks down."

The young men dropped them to the sand, and stood breathing hard.

"Run up the mountain trail, turn back at the top."

They started to run toward us, and I spoke to Kekoa. "They should drink water."

"Take water with you." He yelled out.

Kekoa and I sat by the fire pit.

He looked at me, and asked, "I want to ask you what I would ask the holy man."

I sat up straight, and nodded at him.

"Will we travel safely back to the new village?"

I took in a big breath, and closed my eyes. I saw their boats coming in on the waves, and villagers on the sand welcomed them.

"Yes."

"Will you bring Milana back after her grandfather passes?"

I looked at him, and closed my eyes. Yet I saw nothing.

"I do not know."

He looked at me, "We need a medicine man on the new island."

"I will think on this." I said.

"I will ask the holy man of this." Kekoa said.

When he said this, I felt a strong feeling come over me, and thought, "The holy man will send me away."

I looked into the fire, and the small flames that rose up.

"I do not want to leave." I thought, "I have a family here." and I thought of Konani and the holy man, then my father and my brothers. I liked traveling around this island, and if I joined with Milana, we would be happy here.

"You will go where you are needed." my teacher whispered.

Kekoa stood up, and stretched his big arms over his head. Then with a quick move, he knocked me off the log where I sat, jumped on me and held my arms down.

I spit sand out of my mouth, "What..." I started to ask.

He leaned his head back, and laughed loudly, so that all the villagers could hear.

"You want to train?" he asked, jumped to his feet, and reached out his hand to help me up.

"You have started your training." he told me.

I grabbed one of the sticks his men dropped on the sand, stood back with a fierce look on my face, ready to fight.

Kekoa put his hands on his hips, and shook his head.

Milana walked up from behind Kekoa, and looked at me.

"What is this?"

"He will be trained as a warrior." Kekoa told her.

Milana looked up at Kekoa and smiled, then ran to me, and dropped down to roll into my legs. I fell back on to the sand, she jumped on top of me, with the stick now in her hands.

"I will protect you." she said, and laughed.

Kekoa laughed again, as his men returned, to see Milana sitting on me. There was much laughter, and I felt my face grow hot. I pushed Milana off, stood up and brushed sand from my arms.

"You are strong," Kekoa said, "and will learn fast."

I looked down at Milana, who smiled at me. Her eyes sparkled, and I could not look away.

"She will protect you!" said one of the young men, and they laughed. I turned to see them, and they also watched Milana.

"She is wanted by many men." I thought.

"I will go with Kai," Kekoa told his men. "you will train while I travel."

His men nodded their heads.

"If I do not return, you will leave when the moon is big, and return to the new village."

Milana looked at Kekoa, "Why do you say this?"

"Our village needs fish, and warriors to protect it."

Milana nodded.

"Also, I do not know when the ancestors will take this old man." he said, and smiled.

"You travel with a medicine man." She looked at me.

"I will protect him!" I said, and we laughed again.

I DREAMED MUCH, my sleep was bad, and awoke when the sun started to rise above the mountain. I felt uneasy, and walked to the fire pit. Poking with a stick, I made the hot wood in the fire pit fall apart, and saw it burn brightly.

"What do I feel?" I asked my teacher.

"You are feeling what will come." she told me.

"What will come?"

"Watch and listen." she said.

"I do not like this feeling."

She said no more, and I knew I must not know what comes.

Sunlight was filling the village, and I heard voices coming from the huts. Kekoa and I will leave after we eat, and go to the mountain village. If the boy's mother has passed, I will take him to the holy man. If she has not passed, the boy will stay with her, and I will leave to speak with the holy man about having a new assistant.

"I will do what is needed." I said out loud.

"Good!" Kekoa said from behind me, and now stepped up to face the fire pit.

I laughed, "Are you ready to travel?"

"I am happy to travel this day." he said, "Eat." and handed me a fruit.

We ate, and talked of the trail we would follow.

"I will speak to my men," he said, "you tell Milana of our plans."

I looked at him, and he spoke, "She is your assistant."

I nodded, "I will."

I walked to Milana's grandfather's hut, and heard laughing.

"Welcome!" her grandfather said.

I walked in, and saw Milana pouring tea from a pot.

"Tea?"

"Yes."

Her grandfather waved me to sit by him, and Milana gave us both tea.

"I will travel with Kekoa today."

She looked at me, and nodded.

"I will begin teaching you when I return."

She smiled, "Good." then looked at her grandfather. "The tea you gave him, helps him sleep. I want to learn how to make these medicines."

"This tea is good." I told her.

"It is from the new island."

I finished my tea, and stood. "Thank you."

"Travel well." her grandfather said.

"Travel well." she said, and turned away.

CHAPTER 5

Kekoa and I walked out of the village, up to the high trail on the mountain. Kekoa led, and I took big steps to stay behind him. He stretched his legs far out in front of him, and swung his arms. He carried a basket and bedroll, which looked small on his large back. He talked and laughed, and enjoyed the walk. Kekoa wanted to surprise the holy man, and I would surprise him with a new assistant.

"It is good to be back on this island!" Kekoa said.

"It is good to have you here!"

"Who is the boy in the mountain village?" Kekoa asked.

"A woman asked me to take her son from the village, after she passed."

Kekoa looked at me, "He did not ask to be your assistant?"

"No."

"Why does she want this?"

"He does not have the sickness, and she wants him to live where he can be happy."

"I have seen this sickness." Kekoa said, and shook his head, "a man with it came into my old village, and he was told to leave."

"The mother wants her son to find a woman in another village, and start a new life." I told him.

"We will see if she has passed." Kekoa said.

"Yes, the boy told his mother that he would leave after she had passed, and I told her, I would take him to the flat lands to learn medicine."

"What has the holy man said about this boy?"

"He does not know of him."

"Oh!" Kekoa roared with laughter, "this will be a good surprise!"

"It is hard to surprise the holy man," I said.

Kekoa laughed, "We will see!"

We followed the trail around the mountain, high above the water.

"The big birds fly." Kekoa pointed to birds, with large wings, drifting on the wind not far from us. Suddenly a bird dipped to one side, and flew straight down.

"He hunts!" Kekoa shouted, and stopped to watch.

We watched it fly down the mountain side, until it went behind trees.

"I want to fly like that bird!" Kekoa said.

We both laughed, and Kekoa walked fast ahead of me.

"With you leading, we will get there soon!"

We ate and drank as we walked, and Kekoa told me of the new island. We laughed much, and the sun traveled over our heads quickly.

"It is good to travel with you." I told him.

"You have grown into a good man." Kekoa said, "you are welcome in the new village."

I listened, and felt the holy man would tell me to go with Kekoa to the new island.

"You would like the new island." he told me.

"I am happy on this island." I said, "yet the holy man could tell me to leave."

Kekoa stopped, and turned to look at me.

"He will tell you?"

I looked at him, then out to the sea. "The ancestors tell the holy man where I will go. I have known this since I was young."

"I did not know this."

"The holy man sent other assistants to another island."

"Where?"

"I was told they live on the same island, yet I do not know where."

Kekoa pushed his hair back from his face, and tied it with a string. He was quiet, and thought on this. We started to walk again, I started to sing, and Kekoa sang with me.

The sun was now near the water, and I looked ahead, for my father's village.

"We will see my father's village soon." I told him.

"Good." he said, "I am ready to eat hot fish!"

"There!" I pointed down to fishing boats resting on the sand.

Many trees grew, and a small river ran down from the mountain along the side of the village. We walked under the trees, and Kekoa looked around.

"This is a good village." Kekoa said, "why do you not live here?"

"I am happy to live with the holy man on the flat lands. Also, Konani is my brother, and he lives there with his family."

"I will not tell the holy man we need a medicine man on the new island." he told me.

"The ancestors guide me," I said, "I will go where I am needed."

Kekoa nodded, and we walked into the village.

THE VILLAGERS ENJOYED KEKOA, and he spoke long of leaving, traveling to the new island, then coming back again. He told my father and brothers of when he saw me as a boy, at the medicine man camp, and how he trained Konani.

Kekoa licked his fingers, "The fish is good!" he told the women. They liked watching him eat, and gave him more. He ate more than other men.

"My belly is full!" he said, stretched his arms up, and stood. The villagers sitting around the fire stopped talking, and watched him.

"I will sleep." Kekoa said, and looked at me.

"We will leave when the sun rises." I told my father.

"Sleep well" they called to us, and we walked away to the palm trees, where our bed rolls and baskets sat.

"I enjoyed the fish!" Kekoa said as we walked.

"You did!" I laughed, thinking of the many fish he had eaten.

We stretched our blankets over the sand, Kekoa lay down, and rolled on his side.

I laid down, and looked up at the night sky. I put my hands behind my head, and wondered if Milana was also laying on the sand, looking up at the sky.

"Do you think Milana is ready to join with a man?" I asked Kekoa.

He did not answer, I looked over at him, and heard his breath coming in and out with sleep. I also turned on my side, and closed my eyes.

WHEN THE SUN ROSE, we ate quickly. Jatu put his hand on my shoulder,

"I am glad to see you."

"I am glad to see you." I said, and put my hand on his shoulder. We smiled, then he pushed my chest, I fell back on my other brother, who grabbed me and held my arms like he did when we were children.

Jatu softly punched me in the belly. "Come back, and fish with us."

My brother let go of me, "Yes, fish with us."

"You catch the fish," I told them, "I will come back and eat them!"

We laughed, Kekoa and my father stopped talking, to look at us.

"We must go." I told Kekoa, and we walked from the village, waving back to my family.

"You are welcomed at many villages." Kekoa said.

I did not speak.

"I know why you do not want to leave." he said.

"I will be where the ancestors need a medicine man."

"And a holy man." Kekoa said.

He looked at me, "You also speak to the ancestors."

When I traveled to the villages, I blessed the villagers, and called on the ancestors. I did not think of myself as a holy man, I thought of myself as a medicine man, yet I knew the villagers now called me a holy man.

WE WALKED ON THE SAND, and I pointed to the sea cave, where the young father and mother had hidden with their baby.

"They traveled far from their village." he said.

"They did not stop at my father's village, they let no one see them."

"He hid his family well." Kekoa said, and looked up at the cave.

"When the chief's son and his men walked this way, the young family climbed up the cliff, hid in the trees and ran away."

Kekoa nodded, "Good."

I pointed further down the cliff, to another trail that led up into the trees.

"That trail leads to the flat lands, and where the chief's son led his men to battle.

Kekoa looked up, and stopped. "Do we go this way?"

"No, we will travel to another trail that takes us to the mountain village, then down the other side, to the flat lands."

"You know this island well." Kekoa said.

"I have traveled it much."

"I need to rest." he said.

We put our baskets and bedrolls down, Kekoa stretched his legs out, and looked at the sea.

"I enjoy traveling without the warriors." he said, "I do not have to feed them, tell them to start fires, and where to sleep."

"When I travel to the villages," I said, "I fish where I want, and sleep where I want."

Kekoa looked at me, and smiled, "That will stop when you have a family."

We laughed, and I wondered if he heard me ask of Milana.

We watched the waves and sea birds, then I stood.

"We need to go," I told him, "we will not sleep or eat in the mountain village."

"No hot fish?" he asked.

"The sickness." I said.

He stood up. "I am ready."

WE WALKED TO THE TRAIL, that went up the cliff, and into the trees. I pointed to the rocks we had to climb. Waves had washed away the sand under the rocks, and it was high as my shoulders up to the trail.

"Here." Kekoa said, and cupped his hands, so I could step on them up to the trail.

I climbed up to the top, and turned to him.

"Move back!" he called out, then jumped up, and pulled himself to the top with his arms.

"You are strong!" I said.

"I am getting old!"

"You are getting old," I told him, "yet you are the strongest man I know!"

He followed me, as we walked up the trail, under the trees. With the many trees and plants, we lost the cool sea air, and the heat made us hot. I walked fast, and soon reached the area where I walked off the trail, to find the mud for medicine. Kekoa walked behind me, and we reached the bubbling water, hidden behind tall grass.

"What is this?"

"The mud is for medicine." I told him, "Squeeze the water out, and make a ball."

I showed him, and we filled a small basket, inside my big basket.

"This is good." I said, and we started again, for the mountain village.

WE TRAVELED FAST AND QUIETLY, listening to the bird songs.

"I hear children." Kekoa said.

"We will pass the water where women wash clothes, then come to the village."

The trees opened up, we saw women squatting next to the water, and the children playing in it. The women turned to watch us walk by. I waved to them, yet they did not wave back.

"Do they fear us?" Kekoa asked.

Kekoa smiled and waved, "I do not want them to fear me."

We entered the village, and walked to the men, sitting around the fire pit.

"Welcome." an old man said.

We sat down on logs.

"How is the village?" I asked.

"The same." the old man answered, and smiled.

"I have returned to see a woman." I said.

"That was my daughter." a man's voice said behind me. I turned to see the old man that had shown me to his daughter's hut.

"Has she passed?"

"Yes, after you left, she was glad to go. She was happy you would take her son."

"Where is your grandson?"

"He gathers fruit for the sick."

"This is good." Kekoa said.

The old man looked at Kekoa, at Kekoa's large feet and legs, then up to his wide shoulders and strong arms.

"Who are you?" the grandfather asked.

"My name is Kekoa. I am traveling with Kai, to visit the holy man on the flat lands."

"I have not seen a man such as you." the old man said, and again looked him over.

Kekoa laughed, "I am from another island, where I had brothers larger than me!"

"Oh!" the old man laughed, "I would like to see this!"

"I would also" I said.

. . .

We waited for the boy to return, the sun's light was going away, and I wanted to leave soon.

"There he is!" shouted the grandfather.

Kekoa and I turned to see the old man pointed to a small, boney boy walking with large baskets full of fruit.

"Come here!" the grandfather called to the boy.

As the boy walked to us, I saw his skin was tight around the bones of his face, and he did not look well.

"Is he sick?" I asked the grandfather.

"Sick in his heart." he answered, "he feeds others, yet does not eat himself."

The boy came to us, and dropped down the baskets. He did not smile, only looking at me, then at Kekoa.

"I have returned for you." I told him.

He nodded.

My name is Kai, this is Kekoa."

The boy looked back at Kekoa, and said, "I am Laka."

Kekoa stood up, and Laka looked up to see him.

"Are you ready to travel to the flat lands?" Kekoa asked.

Laka looked back at me.

"We must leave soon, while there is still light." I told him.

"I will give this fruit away" his grandfather said, "you go prepare."

Laka shook his head, "I am not ready."

I looked at the grandfather.

"You will leave me now." the old man said, "you will not wait for me to pass."

Laka's eyes filled with water, and he looked away.

"This is what your mother wanted. I cannot pass in peace, if you do not go." his grandfather told him.

Laka looked down, and I felt his heart hurt. Watching his mother pass, then leaving his grandfather, he would have no family.

"We will wait until the sun rises," I said, "yet we must leave at first light."

Laka looked at me, then at his grandfather, "I will go when the sun rises."

His grandfather nodded.

"I will give this fruit to the sick now." Laka said, picked up the baskets and left us.

The grandfather walked behind him.

Kekoa looked at me, "We will stay?"

I nodded, "We will sleep outside the village."

I quickly went to huts, to see if they needed medicines, then returned to the fire pit.

Darkness was falling, and Kekoa looked at me, "Ready?"

"I will speak to Laka." I walked to Laka's hut, he was there with his grandfather.

"Bring your bedroll and water pouch," I told him, "you can also bring some small things that belonged to your mother."

His eyes looked around the hut.

"Your mother will go with you to the new village," I said, "she will watch over you."

"I will be ready." He told me, and looked at his grandfather.

Kekoa and I left the village and walked into the trees close by. We sat down, and ate dried fish.

"I did not think I would be eating this!" Kekoa said.

I laughed at the face he made, "You will feast on the flat lands."

Kekoa smiled big, "I will enjoy that!"

We made a small fire, and lay down on either side of it.

"You will hear voices," I told him, "the ancestors of this village do not rest well."

"Let them speak," he said, "I will not hear them." He closed his eyes, and soon slept.

THE SUN ROSE, light streaked down through the trees, to find my face. I opened my eyes, looked over at Kekoa, who sat on his bed roll eating a fresh fruit. He picked up a fruit near him, and threw it at me, hitting me in the chest.

"Get up!" he said, and laughed.

I ate the fruit, then looked around, "I must bring back tea leaves."

I knew where to find the dark leaves, and soon filled a small basket.

"Konani enjoys this tea!" I told Kekoa, who had also been picking the leaves.

"I enjoy your work!" he said, "picking leaves, and making mud balls!"

We both laughed, and walked back to the village.

Laka was waiting by the fire pit, with his bed roll, and a basket. His grandfather stood next to him, speaking to him.

"Make a strong hut, and find a good wife." the old man told him.

Laka put his hand on his grandfather's arm. "Can you not come with us?"

"I will come after I have passed. I will come with your mother to see you."

Laka nodded.

"Are you ready?" Kekoa asked Laka.

"Yes." he said.

"Travel well." the grandfather said, and patted Laka on the arm, "Go now."

Laka looked again, into the old man eyes, and turned away. I watched as Laka and Kekoa walked across the clearing of the village, then I looked at the old man.

"I will watch him as a brother." I told him.

The grandfather had water in his eyes, and smiled. "Thank you for doing this." he pointed to Laka and Kekoa, "Go."

I turned, and walked quickly to catch up to Kekoa and Laka, who were already into the trees.

LAKA WAS AHEAD OF US, yet I could feel his heart. I thought of when I left my village, after mother passed. Laka had lost his mother, and now his grandfather. He had no other family, I knew that I would be his new brother, just as Konani had been to me. I wanted to make Laka smile, and began to sing an old song from my childhood.

Suddenly I heard a big voice sing with me, it was Kekoa! We sang loudly and laughed at our own voices.

"You sound like a sick bird!" Kekoa told to me.

I reached down, grabbed a fruit that had fallen on the ground, and threw it at Kekoa.

The ripe fruit flew over his shoulder, and hit Laka on his back.

"What is this?" he cried, and turned quickly to face us.

Kekoa and I stopped, looked at him with open mouths, not knowing what Laka would do. We watched, as he quickly grabbed fruit and threw them at us, then ran down the trail laughing.

Kekoa and I looked at each other.

"He will heal." I said.

Kekoa nodded, and turned to run after Laka.

Laka led us down the mountain trail, until we reached the cliff, looking at the sea.

"Have you been here?" I asked him.

"I came here to look at the sea, yet did not leave the mountain."

We stood side by side, looking out over the sand and water.

"We will eat on the sand." I told them.

"I will get fresh fish." Kekoa said.

We climbed down the rocks of the cliff, and walked on the sand, to the water. Kekoa put down his basket and bed roll, and pulled his sharp blade from a pouch, that hung from his waist. Laka and I watched Kekoa climb on rocks, then dive into the water as a wave rolled in.

"He is strong!" Laka said.

"Yes, he is a warrior and teaches others to fight."

"I would not want to fight him!" Laka said.

We watched Kekoa swimming on top of the water, then diving under it with the blade in his mouth. Soon he held up a fish speared on the blade, and he began to swim back.

"We will make a fire." I told Laka, and we gathered small, dry pieces of wood, and put them in a pile.

Kekoa walked to us, "We do not need a fire!"

He pulled the fish off the blade, and held it out to us, "This is good cold."

Kekoa used his blade, to cut fish from the bone, and handed us a piece of fish.

"Eat!" he said, and put fish into his mouth, "This is good!"

I also put the fish in my mouth, yet Laka held his, and looked at us.

"Why do you not eat?" Kekoa asked.

"I have not eaten fish from the sea."

"You will eat many fish from the sea." I told him, "they are eaten hot and cold."

"Eat!" Kekoa said in a loud voice.

Laka put the fish into his mouth. He chewed slowly, then smiled, "This is good!"

Kekoa laughed and slapped Laka on the back. "You will grow strong eating this fish!"

Kekoa cut more fish for us, and we enjoyed the taste of the fresh fish.

"You will feast at the village." I told Laka.

"I will be glad to taste new foods."

"And I will also!" Kekoa said, and ate the last bite of fish.

We drank water, and began to walk along the water, toward the flat lands. Kekoa and I told Laka of the holy man, and Konani. I told him of the holy man's brothers, their families, and of Maleko and his family.

"There are many!" Laka said.

"They will be glad to see you." I said.

Kekoa looked at me and smiled. We knew that Laka was a surprise!

CHAPTER 6

We traveled along the sand, and Laka wanted to know of the sea plants, and fish. Kekoa told Laka of these, while Laka ran to keep up with Kekoa's long steps. I walked behind, and wondered if Laka would find his woman on the flat lands. I thought of Konani, and the chief's son, when they walked on this trail. Konani traveled to see the woman he would join with, and the chief's son traveled to where he would pass in battle.

"Enjoy this," my teacher said, "we do not know what is on the trail ahead."

"I could pass to the ancestors!" I said, "when the holy man learns I have brought a new assistant to stay with him, and have another I will return to."

Kekoa stopped, and looked back at me. "Are you speaking?"

I laughed, "I speak to my teacher!"

Kekoa laughed, "How long before I see the holy man?"

I looked up at the sun, which had started to travel down, "Soon."

"Good!" Kekoa said, then turned, and started to walk faster.

Laka looked at Kekoa, then back at me. "I will walk with you."

. . .

"My eyes see far down here." Laka said.

"See far?" I asked.

"In my village, I saw the trees."

I nodded.

"Down here I look far over the water, or see ahead on the sand. My eyes like this."

I thought of what he said, "I also like to look across the water."

"I like this place." he said.

"Look!" Kekoa yelled.

We looked where he pointed out to sea, and saw a boat, so far away it looked small.

"We are near!" I yelled back.

Kekoa stopped, and looked back at me. I pointed to the boat, a big smile came across his face, he turned and began to run.

Kekoa was soon far ahead of us. I could have run with him, yet I knew Laka could not.

"Do you want me to carry your basket or bed roll?"

He stopped, and looked up at me with an angry face. "I do not need help!"

I pulled my head back, and looked at him.

"When I was a boy, and left my village, Konani carried my bedroll."

"I am not a boy!" he said, "I can carry my own bedroll!"

He began to walk away from me, so I took quick steps to walk beside him.

"Do not be angry!" I said, "I want to help."

"I am small," he said, "yet I can care for myself."

"I see this." I told him, "if you need help, I am sure you will ask."

Laka did not look at me, "No one has helped me."

I put my hand on his shoulder, and he stopped walking.

"We help each other here."

He looked at me, and water came into his eyes. He said nothing, and nodded his head. We started to walk again, and I thought it was hard for Laka. He did not have a father, no brothers and sisters, his mother was sick, and his grandfather was old.

"He took care of himself." I thought.

"His heart is behind a wall." my teacher whispered.
"I want him to be happy." I thought.
We did not see Kekoa ahead of us, he left us to walk behind.
"You will like the flat lands." I told him.
"Why do you say this?"
"You will see many new villagers."
He did not speak.
"When I left my village, I did not know where I would go, or what I would do."
Laka looked at me, "You did not know?"
I smiled at him, "The holy man told me I would learn to make medicines, yet I did not know, that the holy man and Konani would be my new family."
"I do not need a new family!" he said.
I did not know why he was angry.
"His heart needs to heal." my teacher said.

WE WALKED DOWN THE SAND, and I did not speak more of this. The sun was low to the water when we reached the trail to Konani's hut, and the trail to the holy man's hut.
We stopped, I pointed to the trail going up, and told him that Konani and Maleko lived there.
"We go there." I pointed to the trail going across the flat lands.
"The flat lands are big." he said.
"There are many villages here."
We heard Kekoa's laugh louder than the others, and I saw them, standing around the fire pit.
"Hey!" I yelled, and put my arms in the air, to wave at them.
They turned to look, and yelled back. The children ran to us, shouting, "Kai, Kai!"
I looked at Laka, and his eyes were big, as he looked around.
Konani walked to us, and put his hand on my shoulder, "Welcome!"
"I am happy to be back." I turned to look at Laka, "This is Konani."
Laka looked at him, and said, "I am Laka."

"Welcome." Konani said, reaching behind Laka, to grab the basket from his back.

Laka was surprised, and held his basket on his shoulders, "I can carry it." he said.

"You have traveled far, let me carry it now." Konani told him.

Laka looked at me.

I smiled and said, "We help each other."

We walked to the fire pit, and I brought Laka to the holy man.

"This is Laka." I said, and looked at the holy man.

"Does he know why Laka is here?" I thought.

"The new assistant!" Kanoa shouted.

Kanoa, Hiapo, Mano and Aukai walked to him and clapped him on the back and arms. Laka looked at each brother, and nodded.

I knew that Kekoa had told them of Laka, I looked at Kekoa, and he smiled at me.

The brothers' women brought fruit, and fresh fish cooked on the fire. It smelled good.

The holy man stood, raised his arms, and we got quiet.

"Thank you Father for this good day, for bringing Kekoa, Kai and Laka to feast with us."

I looked at Laka, and he watched the holy man carefully.

"Thank you Mother for giving us this food. We ask the ancestors to feast with us this night."

"Yes!" cried out Aukai, "We thank you."

The families talked, laughed, and passed the fruit and fish around.

"Laka, do you fish?" Kanoa asked.

"I have fished in the stream, on the mountain."

"You will fish with us on the sea!" Mano said.

Laka's eyes opened big, and he smiled. "I would like that."

I ate much, then looked across the fire at the holy man. I stood, and walked around to him.

"Walk with me?" I asked.

We walked away from the fire pit, going toward the sea.

"You have brought a new assistant." he said.

"Did you know of him?"

"I dreamed of him."

"His mother asked me to take him from the mountain village."

"She lives with the ancestors." he said.

I looked at him, wondered what he knew, and did not tell me.

"I will take him to the medicine man's camp." he said.

"I will go back for another assistant." I told him.

He looked at me, "Kekoa told me of her."

"She will live with her grandfather, while I train her."

"He will pass," the holy man said, "and she will return to the new island."

"Yes."

I looked at him, and wanted him to tell me if I would leave also.

"We will travel together," he said, "I will meet this woman."

"Good."

We stood and looked at the water. The sun had gone down, yet light still lit the sky and clouds.

"We will let the boy rest, feed him, and make him strong."

The holy man turned to me, and put his hand on my shoulder, "See Konani."

HE TURNED and walked back to the fire pit, I watched him go, then looked across the water.

I closed my eyes, felt the cool air from the sea, and heard the waves crashing. I felt peace in my heart, and was glad to be back.

"I will give Konani his tea." I thought, and turned to walk back.

I saw Konani sitting closely to Lelani, with children on their laps, and the others sitting next to them. He smiled and laughed. Leilani cared for him well, and was a good mother to his children.

"He is happy." I thought.

I stood at the fire pit, and watched them.

"I am happy also." I thought, yet wondered how it would feel to join with a woman, and make a family. I watched them, and thought of Milana.

"Will I join with her?"

She made me think of this, and I wondered what a child with her would look like.

"I could build a hut here, and raise up my family by Konani."

"Kai."

I looked away from Konani, and saw the holy man.

"I will sleep, bring Laka to the hut when you are ready." he told me.

I nodded, and looked around for Laka. He sat talking with Aukai's son. I walked over, and heard them speaking of fishing.

"Laka."

They stopped talking, and looked at me. "We will sleep in the holy man's hut. When you are ready, bring your bedroll and basket."

"Where is the holy man's hut?" he asked.

Aukai's son spoke up, "I will show you."

"Good." I said, and the boys began talking again.

I saw Konani standing, and walked to him.

"I have mountain tea for you."

"Bring it to me when the sun rises," he smiled, "we will drink tea, and I will hear of your travels."

"I have much to tell you."

"Good." he said.

He left with Lelani, and their children.

"My body is tired." I thought, "I will sleep also."

I SLEPT WITHOUT DREAMS, and awoke when the sun lit the inside of the hut. I looked around to see the holy man had gone, and Laka still sleeping on his bedroll. I got up, grabbed the mountain tea from my basket, and left without waking Laka. The holy man sat by the fire pit drinking tea, and I walked to him.

"I take tea to Konani."

"Good." he said, "I will speak with Laka."

I left for Konani's hut, and began to run. I wanted to enjoy sitting with him, drinking tea, and telling him of Milana.

"You run!" he yelled.

I laughed, and soon joined him at his fire pit.

"I am ready for tea!" Konani said, as I gave it to him.

He put it in a pot of water sitting on the fire.

"I have watched you make tea since I was a boy!"

"When will you make my tea!" he called out, and laughed.

He pointed to the fruit trees, and they had much fruit.

"I need more trees to put in the dirt." he told me.

"Those trees have many fruit!" I said.

"My children are growing, Lelani told me to get more trees."

"I will help you." I told him.

Konani used a palm leaf to lift the hot pot from the fire, and pour tea into our shells.

"Now," he said, and sat down next to me, "tell me of this woman that will be your new assistant."

I told him of Milana, and her grandfather, then looked at him.

"I think of joining with her."

"She wants to join with you?"

"I do not know."

"You have not spoken to her of this?"

"No," I told him, "I spoke only of teaching her medicine."

Konani shook his head.

"She is a warrior," I told him, "she is not like other women."

He took in a big breath, blew it out, and I knew his teacher spoke to him.

"Be her teacher, let her know you."

I nodded.

"She will tell you what she wants." he said.

"I will wait for her to be ready."

He laughed, "You are not ready!"

I told him of Laka, "It is good that he left the mountain village."

"The holy man needs a new assistant." Konani told me.

"Why do you say this?"

"He needs to teach, he needs to stop sitting at the fire pit, like an old man!"

We laughed hard.

"I take medicine to the villages on the flat lands," he said, "you travel around the island to give medicine, and the holy man eats and talks with his brothers!"

"He will take Laka to the old camp." I told him.

"Will you carry his basket?" Konani asked, and we laughed more.

I enjoyed seeing Konani, the holy man, the brothers and all the women and children. Maleko came with his woman to see me and the new assistant. I felt welcomed, and I felt they were my family. I swam each day in the sea, ran on the trails to stay strong, and was glad to be back.

Laka smiled more, and enjoyed the young men and women in the village. He left each day with them to walk on the sand, and swim in the waves, at night he sat talking with them at the fire pit. He told the holy man that he wanted to learn of plants, and to make medicine. I felt he would be a good assistant, and the holy man thought this also.

I STOOD, dripping water from my swim, and watched the sea birds fly low over the waves.

"Kai." I turned to see the holy man walking to me.

"We will leave when the sun rises."

I nodded. I was ready to see Milana again.

"We will travel with Kekoa and Laka, then take Laka and the girl to the old camp."

"Good." I said.

The medicine man looked out to the sea, "They must learn fast, as you did."

"Why do you say this?"

"The ancestors have shown me dark clouds, and a big boat."

"Big boat?"

"A boat from another island." He said, and was not happy.

"Are these warriors?"

"I do not know, yet my heart hurts."

"What will we do?"

"We will teach Laka and the girl."

"Milana." I said.

"You will teach Milana, I will teach Laka."

"What of the boat?" I asked

"I do not know, yet I feel these dark clouds coming."

"I have felt a new life coming."

He looked at me, "You will have this soon."

My mouth fell open a little, I started to speak, then he put his hand on my shoulder.

"I will tell Kekoa and Laka we leave." Then he walked away.

"What kind of new life will I have?" I asked my teacher, yet no answer came.

I wanted to speak with Konani, of what the holy man said, yet he had left to give medicines. I wondered if Konani knew of the boat, or dark clouds coming. I cut leaves from the medicine plants next to the holy man's hut, cleaned out my basket and packed dried fish and fruit into it, along with the medicine plants. I was ready to travel, and still the sun was high in the sky. I stood looking at the mountain, thinking of what to do, when I saw Konani's hut up the trail.

"I will plant new fruit trees for him!"

I smiled to myself, this would be a good surprise. I grabbed a large blade from the holy man's hut, and started for the mountain. I ran fast up the trail, passing Maleko and Konani's huts on my way. I enjoyed feeling my strong body carry me up the trail. My bare feet gripped the dirt, pushing me forward, and my arms swung like arrows going back and forth beside me. My body was getting warm under the sun, my breathing getting deeper, and I was quickly coming to the trees. I slowed down, ran off the trail, and stopped if front of them. I looked around for small trees growing by their mother, and walked into the shade. There were many kinds of trees here, yet I did not see any with fruit. I heard water, and walked toward it. I saw a small stream, bent down and splashed the cool water on my face, then took a drink.

"Thank you Father and Mother." I said out loud.

I looked at the sky, stretched my arms up, and closed my eyes. I heard the water moving over the rocks in the stream, and birds speaking. I took in a big breath, and blew it out. Peace slowly came down on me, and I let my arms fall down to my sides.

"Feel this" my teacher whispered, "think of this when you need peace."

I felt my feet standing on the dirt, and the small wind blow across my body. My heart was happy, and my thoughts had peace.

I nodded my head, "I will think of this."

I walked through the trees, and looked much, to find fruit that Konani did not have growing by his hut. I dug the small trees carefully from the dirt, with the sharp blade, and put them on my shoulders to carry back.

Lelani sat outside the hut, weaving a mat, and watching her children play.

"I found trees for you."

She smiled, put the mat down, and slowly stood.

"You grow a child?"

She smiled, "It is small, yet my body feels it."

"Konani grows a large family!" I said, and was happy for him.

The children saw me, and ran to see the trees. Leilani looked at them, felt their leaves, and nodded her head.

"I do not have these."

"I wanted new fruit for the children." I told her.

"Fruit!" the children cried out, and followed me.

Leilani and the children watched me dig the dirt, and put them into it.

"Thank you Kai."

"I will give them water."

She pointed to the pot, that gathered water from the sky.

After pouring water around the new trees, I put my hands by each.

"Grow well." I told them.

She smiled, "Konani will be surprised, and happy."

"Tell him we leave when the sun rises."

"I will, are you hungry?

I was hungry, yet wanted to return to my hut. "No. Tell Konani I will bring back tea."

She smiled, "Travel safe brother."

The sun was lower when I returned to camp. Aukai and Kanoa were back from fishing, and their women were cutting fruit, and preparing other plants to eat. I sat on a log by the fire pit, and listened to Aukai and Kanoa tell Haipo and Mano of their fishing. I watched them, their families, and suddenly felt I would not see them again. My heart hurt.

"Why is this?" I thought, "are the ancestors leading me away?"

I looked at the brothers, their women and children, and wondered if they felt this, yet I knew they did not.

"Why do I feel this, and others do not?

"You watch your feelings carefully." my teacher said, "You also listen to your inner voice."

"They do not?" I asked.

"Their inner voice is quiet, they must learn to hear it."

THE HOLY MAN, Laka and I stood by the fire pit, with the sun just beginning to light the darkness around us. We sipped our tea and ate fresh fruit. I wondered why I had not seen Konani last night.

"He must have taken the high trail home." I thought. I had wanted to speak with him of what the holy man said.

"We will stay at Kai's old village, then go to the next village, where we will get another assistant." the holy man said.

"Another assistant?" Laka asked.

"Yes, a girl, her name is," the holy man stopped speaking, and looked at me.

"Milana"

"Then we go to the old camp. This is where you will learn to make medicine."

Laka nodded.

"Are you ready?" I asked them.

"Yes." Laka spoke up.

"Yes." the holy man said.

We went back to the hut, put the baskets and bedrolls on our backs, and walked to the trail barely lit by the new sun.

We traveled quickly, Laka was much stronger, and kept with us. I led, then Laka, and the holy man followed. We passed Konani's hut, and he waved to us from his firepit.

"Thank you for the fruit trees!" he yelled.

"I will bring you tea!" I yelled back.

The trail went up, and I did not slow. I heard Laka behind me, and when we got to the trail that led up into the mountain, I stopped. I turned and Laka stepped up beside me, together we looked down the trail, to see the holy man had fallen behind. When he reached us, he breathed hard.

He stopped in front of us, and breathed in and out deeply.

"I have gotten old!"

"You need to walk more, and eat less!" I said, and pointed my finger at his round belly.

He looked down, and laughed.

Laka also laughed.

We waited for the holy man to travel again, and I looked down on the village by the water.

"My village." I thought.

"I am ready."

"You go ahead." I told him, and he led us on to the trail.

We walked through the mountain, and beside the stream. I sang old songs, and the holy man sang with me.

"Do you not know these songs?" I asked Laka.

"No." he answered

"Listen and learn them." I told him.

"I am not a singer."

"Sing! And we will tell you if you are a singer!" the holy man said.

I laughed, yet Laka was quiet.

"I will wait for you to surprise us with a song!" I said.

We traveled on, and the holy man stopped, when he saw plants that he used for medicine. He told Laka of them, yet did not pick them.

"We will gather plants at the old camp." he said.

With the holy man leading, and stopping to talk of plants, we did not travel fast as I would have. I watched the sun travel above our heads, and wondered when we would hear sea birds, and smell the water again. We reached the end of the trail, where we looked out on the water, and I was happy.

"We will not stop." the holy man said, as he started to climb down the cliff.

Laka followed him, and I stood to see the water in front of me. Watching the water move up and down, rolling into waves that crashed, and pushed the water on to the sand. I did not grow tired of watching this. I saw the holy man walking with Laka close behind, and I climbed down the rocks quickly, then jumped to the sand.

We traveled by the water, came to rocks, climbed over them, then walked again on the sand. This was the sea trail, and I was glad to follow it. The sounds of the waves crashing, and the birds crying over head, made me think of how Mother lives in these also. Each rock, each wave, the birds and each shell on the sand.

"Mother is great." I thought.

"We will eat." the holy man said, and he pointed to a place shaded by trees.

While we ate, I asked Laka how he liked staying on the flat lands.

"I like it much."

"You will also like the old medicine man's camp."

"Tell me of this."

The holy man told Laka of the medicine men, that have used the camp since the ancestors built it.

"There are many plants on the mountain, that we will use to make medicines," the holy man said, "we will gather these each day."

Listening to him speak, made me think of when I traveled to the old camp, and how Konani and the holy man taught me.

"I am blessed." I thought, "I have been well cared for, and I am thankful."

. . .

We entered my father's village as the sun was sitting on the water, and soon sat at the fire pit, joined by my father, brothers and old friends. They wanted to know of the other villages, and the holy man told them much, to make them laugh. Laka listened, laughing with the others, while I quietly walked to the water. I wanted to swim, yet the big fish eat when the sun is low, so I walked into the water and splashed myself.

"I will swim at Milana's village." I thought.

I wanted to rise with the sun, and walk quickly to see her, yet I had to travel with the holy man and Laka. Konani and the holy man had traveled slowly with me as a boy, even taking my pack. I laughed, I had been a boney boy then, like Laka.

"I wonder how Milana will learn from me."

I saw her face, and her strong body. She was a warrior, and did not like men telling her what to do.

"I am strong," I thought, "yet teaching this small woman gives me a little fear!"

I kicked the sand in front of me, and looked around. Flames from the fire now rose high, I saw the dark shadows of villagers, sitting and standing around the firepit.

"I will let the ancestors guide me." I told myself, and walked back to join my father and brothers.

CHAPTER 7

I rose as the sun came up, and walked to the fire pit, where my brothers and father already sat. My brothers would fish this day, and my father liked to watch them take the boat out to sea.

"Leaving?" my father asked.

"Yes, we go to the grandfather's village, then to the old medicine camp on the mountain."

"Travel well." my father said.

I looked down at his old face, and I wondered if I would see him again.

"Enjoy this day, and eat many fish!" I said, and looked at my brothers.

"We will catch many!"

"And eat them!" Jatu said.

We laughed, and I saw the holy man and Laka coming to join us.

We ate and drank tea, then watched my brothers walk to their boats. I waved at them, and looked back at my father.

"I thank you for letting me learn medicine."

He smiled, "You did not like to fish."

"I did not."

"I am happy that you make medicine, and help the villages." he told me.

I put my hand on his shoulder, "You are a good father."

He was surprised by this, and his face changed suddenly, with water coming into his eyes.

"Go now!" he said, and clapped me on the arm.

I looked at the holy man, who had been watching us.

"We will leave." He told us.

WE LEFT my father's village, and I felt that I would not see him, or my brothers again.

I walked quietly, "I have bad feelings," I thought, "yet do not know why."

I wondered why I was feeling this, then I thought her!

"Since Milana returned, I have wanted to be with her! Is that why I will leave, and not see my family again?" I said out loud.

The holy man stopped, he and Laka turned to look at me.

I stopped and shook my head.

"You will see your brothers again." the holy man said.

I took in a big breath, "Thank you."

Laka looked from me to the holy man. He did not know of what we spoke.

The holy man turned, walked away, with Laka following. I stood there not moving.

"Help me!" I thought to my teacher.

"You have traveled a path you know," she said, "now you feel a new path coming."

"It does not feel good."

"You do not know where this path leads," she said, "and you have fear."

I thought of this, "Yes, I fear what I do not know, and I feel the ancestors push me."

"The ancestors do not push you," she said, "your inner teacher pushes you."

"Oh." I was surprised, "my inner teacher."

THE SUN ROSE, traveled over us, then went down to the sea. I thought much of walking a new path, and did not want this. I wanted to stay on this island, I liked living on the flat lands. I wanted to join with a woman, grow a family, and be an old man with Konani. I saw us sitting at the fire pit laughing, and talking of when we were young. Then Laka stopped in front of me, we had reached the trail that looked over the grandfather's village.

"I will see Milana," I thought, yet I was not glad as before.

We walked into the village, and heard shouts coming from the sand. I walked quickly to them, saw Kekoa yelling at his warriors, as they fought with their spears. I looked for Milana, and saw her fiercely fighting, with a young man much bigger than her.

"That is Milana!" I told the holy man, and pointed to her.

"She has a strong spirit." he said.

Kekoa turned to see us.

"Welcome!" he shouted, then turned back to the warriors, "Run!"

They dropped their spears and started running past us, up the trail we just came down. We watched Milana run by, and she looked straight ahead.

"Welcome old friend!" Kekoa said, and clapped the holy man on the back.

"Your warriors are strong, and prepared to fight." the holy man said.

"I do not want to fight," Kekoa said, "yet they are prepared."

"This is good." the holy man said, "The ancestors have shown me much."

Kekoa looked down at him, and nodded, "Come."

They walked away, and I looked at Laka.

"Are you hungry?"

"Yes."

We walked to the fire pit, sat down, and grabbed dried fish from our baskets.

"Eat this." A mother and her daughter handed us a palm leaf, with fresh fruit, and cooked fish.

"Thank you." I said.

Laka was surprised, and looked at the daughter, "Thank you."

They walked away, and he looked at me.

"In your father's village and here, we have been welcomed and fed. Why is this?"

"Our villages welcome travelers, and give them food," I told him, "Yet when the holy man comes, they honor him. They know he will bless the village, and ask the ancestors to protect them."

"They also honor his assistants."

"Yes." I said, and nodded, "They know he teaches us."

WHEN LAKA and I finished eating, I stood up and stretched my arms, then swung them from side to side.

"We will see the villagers and give medicine." I told him.

He stood up, and stretched. "I am ready."

I led him to huts and we were welcomed, yet none needed medicine. I wanted to see Milana's grandfather, and we walked to his hut.

"Welcome!" he shouted to us. He sat, sipping tea.

"How are you?" I asked.

"Good! Milana feeds me well!"

"Good."

"When will you start teaching her?" he asked.

"Soon." I said, "she will go with us to the medicine man's camp."

He nodded. "She needs to learn medicine, not fighting!"

We heard foots steps behind us, and turned to see her walking into the hut. She was hot, and water dripped from her face. Her long black hair was tied back, yet strands stuck to her face and neck.

"Look at you!" her grandfather said, "you are a woman, and should be getting soft for a man!"

I looked at her, and saw what he spoke of. Milana had strong arms and legs. Her stomach was flat and hard, and she stood there, with her hands on her hips.

SPIRIT BY THE SEA TRILOGY

"Grandfather!" she shook her head, and looked at me, "You are back."

"Yes."

"Who is this?" she asked looking at Laka.

I looked at Laka, and he looked at Milana with big eyes.

"This is Laka," I told her, "he will also learn medicine."

She looked down at his feet, then up to his face.

"He will be a new assistant?"

"I will teach you, and the holy man will teach Laka."

"You will teach me?" she said, and turned to look at me.

I nodded, "The holy man will also."

Milana looked back at Laka, "Do you speak?"

Laka's face got hot, "I speak!" he said, and walked out of the hut.

"Milana!" her grandfather said, "do you not know how to welcome a traveler?"

Milana looked at her grandfather, then down at her feet.

"We will travel to the medicine man's camp." I said.

She looked at me, "When will we return?"

"I do not know, you must learn the plants, and how to make medicine."

She looked at her grandfather.

"You go." he said.

She shook her head.

"I want you to learn medicine, not fighting!" he told her.

She walked to him, sat down and put her arm around his shoulder.

He looked into her eyes, "I do not need you to care for me.

"I do not want to leave you again."

He put his hand on her leg, "I will not pass when you are away."

Milana looked at him, and nodded. "I will go."

"Good." he said, and looked at me, "She will be a good assistant."

"Do you need anything?" she asked her grandfather.

"No, I will finish my tea."

"I will swim." she said.

"Go." he said, and pointed to the doorway.

65

She kissed him on the forehead, and did not look at me as she walked out.

I turned to watch her leave, "She is the same angry girl I met on the sand," I thought, "Why is she angry?"

"She feels she must fight," my teacher said, "to be a warrior, to be a medicine woman."

"She is a good fighter!" I thought, and looked back at her grandfather.

"When will you leave?" he asked.

"The holy man will tell us."

He shook his head, "My granddaughter has a good heart, yet she hides it."

I nodded, "I know this."

"She will not let you care for her," he looked at me, "yet watch over her."

"I will," I nodded to him, "I will."

I left his hut, and saw Laka waiting for me. I waved for him to come, and we walked to another hut.

"Welcome" a young mother said to us.

"Can we help you?"

She nodded, and called to her son.

A young boy ran to us, smiling.

"Look." she said, and bent down to grab her son's leg. She held it up, and we saw a hot, swollen wound.

"Is this from swimming?"

He nodded, and looked at his leg.

The boy scratched his leg on a living rock, under the water, and now it tried to grow in him. This happens in all the sea villages, and mothers cut the plant out, then put sea salt on it.

"I have cleaned it, and put salt on it." his mother said, "yet it is still bad."

"I have medicine." I said, and put my basket down to look in. I grabbed leaves, and handed them to the mother.

"Pound these, add a little hot tea, then put them on his leg. When they dry, put more on, and when he sleeps"

She took the leaves in both her hands. "Thank you."

"I will come back." I told her, and reached down to grab my basket.

She took the leaves into the hut, and came out with a large fruit. "Here."

I took it, "Thank you."

She took her son into the hut. and we left.

"What will the leaves do?" Laka asked.

"They draw out the poison, and dry up the wound."

We went to the next hut, where an old woman sat outside. She smiled, and waved us to her.

"Do you need medicine?"

She nodded, and held her hands up. "My hands hurt."

I took her hand, and looked at it. Her fingers looked like old tree branches, with many knots, and they felt warm.

"How long?" I asked her.

"When the clouds come in, before the water falls." she said, and pointed out to the dark clouds, blowing in over the sea.

I grabbed a pouch from my basket. "Make tea, and drink it when your hands are like this."

"Will you make this tea for me?" she asked, "my pot is in the hut."

"Yes." I said, and walked in to get her pot. I looked around, and saw the dirt was wet in the corner.

"Does your hut leak water?" I asked, pointing to the top of her hut.

She nodded.

"We will make tea, and come back." I told her, and walked away with Laka.

"She needs help." I told him.

We put the tea and water into the pot, and sat it on the hot wood of the fire pit.

I then spoke to the men sitting there.

"There is an old woman," and I pointed to her sitting in front of her hut, "her hut is leaking water, and the dirt is wet."

The men stood up, "We will look at this." they said, and walked to her hut.

I looked at Laka, "Not all the old people have family in this village. The young left for a new island."

"That is why you call it "the grandfather's village?" he asked.

"Yes." I said, and told him of the chief's son, and the warriors that traveled to this village.

"I am glad they did not come to my village." Laka said.

"Kekoa trains his warriors to protect the villages." I told him.

"This is good."

The water bubbled, and the tea turned the water dark. "It is ready." I said, and used a palm leaf to take it to the old woman. I poured the tea for her.

"Here" I said, and gave it to her. "Drink all the tea, and your hands will feel better."

"Thank you."

"I left more tea leaves in your hut." I told her, as we walked away.

"You carry many kinds of medicines in your basket." Laka said.

"Feel my basket." I said, and handed it to him.

Laka grabbed it with one hand, and when I let go, the basket dropped to the ground.

"That is heavy!" he cried.

"I made this basket strong to carry many medicines." I told him, and picked it up, "You will also make a strong basket, at the medicine man's camp."

LAKA and I walked to the other huts, then to the fire pit. The wind blew strong over the water, and through the trees. I heard sounds as the leaves stretched and cracked.

"Water will pour down soon." Laka said, holding his hands over the hot wood in the fire.

"Yes, we will find the holy man."

We found the holy man, and Kekoa, sitting in a hut where the warriors sleep.

The holy man looked at us, and Kekoa stood up, "Welcome!"

We walked in, and put our baskets down.

"Water clouds are blowing in." I told them.

"When they have blown over, we will leave." the holy man said.

"Sleep here this night." Kekoa told us.

"I will tell Milana to be prepared, and come back." I said.

The holy man nodded, and looked at Laka. Laka sat on the floor next to him, and I left. Water blew in the air with the wind, and I ran to Milana's grandfather's hut.

"Come!" he said when he saw me.

Milana was bringing him food, and she turned to look at me.

"Welcome," she said and smiled.

I stopped and looked at her. I was surprised by her, again.

"Thank you."

"Are you hungry?"

"Yes."

"Sit." she told me.

She returned to where she had prepared fruit and hot fish, she put it on a palm leaf, and brought it to me.

"Thank you."

She got herself food, and sat by us.

"We will leave after the water clouds blow over." I told her.

"I will be ready."

I watched her eat, and did not take my eyes from her.

"She is beautiful." I thought. She sat cross legged, and her hair fell to the mat. Her skin was smooth, and dark from the sun. I looked at the dark markings on her arm and leg.

"How do you make these?" I asked, and put my hand on her arm.

She stopped eating, and pulled her arm from me. "Kekoa knows an old man that does this."

"Is there pain?" I said, looking at her arm.

"No." she said, and started to eat again.

I looked at her, and knew it hurt, yet she would not tell me.

She suddenly looked at me, "I must gather fruit for grandfather before we leave."

"I will help you." I told her.

"I ate fish and fruit before you came back!" her grandfather said.

Milana looked at him, "I know you are well cared for, yet I want to bring fruit for the hut."

Her grandfather looked at me, "She is like her mother."

I looked at him, then back to Milana. "Does she look like her?"

Her grandfather smiled, "I look at Milana, and see my daughter."

Milana got up, and looked outside. "The water is starting to come down."

I stood up, "I am ready."

I followed her down the trail, used by the villagers, to pick fruit from the trees.

"Here." she said, and pointed up. "I want the new ones, so he can eat them later."

The new fruit was above our heads.

"Help me" she said, put her hand on my shoulder, and lifted her foot up.

I grabbed her foot, and lifted her up, to where she reached a branch, and pulled herself on to it. I watched her arms and legs, they were strong. She was not soft as her grandfather said, yet I liked her body. She picked the fruit, and threw them down. When she finished, she climbed down to me, and I put my arms up to her.

"I will catch you." I told her.

She smiled, and jumped. I caught her and held her to me, with her feet dangling. I felt her against me, and smelled her hair. We both laughed, and I looked in her eyes. She looked away, then put her hands on my chest and pushed. I dropped her, and she gathered up the fruit.

"Thank you." she said, then walked back on the trail, and I stood watching her go.

I still felt her body against mine, and I wanted more. I ran to walk by her.

"Do you have a basket?" I asked.

"No," she said, "I have a bedroll."

"I will come for you, when the holy man wants to leave."

She looked at me, "I will be ready."

"You have been ready since you were a girl!"

She punched me in the arm, and smiled. "I am not a girl now!"

I held my arm, "You are a warrior!"

She stopped smiling, "Yes I am."

While Laka and the holy man still sat at the fire pit, I took my bedroll to the warriors' hut, and lay down. I closed my eyes, and saw Milana. Sitting with her hair touching the mat, eating, climbing the tree, then holding her against me. I smiled, and let sleep come.

CHAPTER 8

I heard the holy man walk out of the hut, I got up, and walked to Laka and shook him. He rubbed his eyes and nodded. I went back to my bed roll, rolled it up, grabbed my basket and walked to the doorway. Outside the sky was dark, and the dirt was wet from water that fell during the night. I looked toward the fire pit, saw Kekoa's large body in front of the fire, so I walked to Milana's hut.

Her bedroll leaned against the door, and she stood next to her grandfather.

"If you need me, send a runner to me." she told him.

He put his hand on her arm, "You go, I am good."

They heard me, and turned to see me.

"We gather at the fire pit." I told them.

Milana nodded and said, "I will be there soon."

I looked at her grandfather, "I will watch over her."

"Good." he said.

I left and walked to the fire pit. Laka was already eating fruit, and the holy man drank tea.

"Where is Milana?" Kekoa asked.

"She comes."

I also ate fruit, and sipped hot tea.

Milana joined us. She carried a bamboo spear, and a basket in her hand. Her bedroll hung from her shoulder.

"Did you eat?" I asked her.

"Yes." she said, and looked at the fire.

"I will return to the new village soon." Kekoa told her.

She looked at him, yet did not speak.

"You will be at the old camp, when I leave." Kekoa said.

She nodded.

"Can you find the new island?" he asked her.

Milana nodded, "Yes."

"I will welcome our new medicine woman."

"I will return," she told him, "and live in the hut I built."

"Build a long boat that travels fast." Kekoa said.

"I will help." I said.

Kekoa looked at me and smiled, "You and Milana will build a good boat."

"We leave." the holy man said, and put his hand on Kekoa's arm, "Travel well to the new village."

Kekoa stood, and looked at the holy man. "Will I see you again old friend?"

"We will see each other again," the holy man smiled, "yet it may be after we pass."

Kekoa nodded, "Travel well, I will see you again!"

He turned to me, and clapped me on the arm, "Take care of my warrior!" he said, and laughed.

He put his hand on Milana's arm, "Learn fast."

She nodded, "I will."

The holy man started down the trail, Laka carried only his bedroll, and was close behind him. I put on my basket, and looked at Milana. She slung her bedroll over her shoulder, and held a basket in her hand.

"I am ready."

We walked away from Kekoa, who stood watching us leave.

. . .

The sun started to peak through the clouds, yet water had made pools on the trail, and we watched where we stepped. Milana traveled ahead of me, and she easily kept up with the holy man and Laka. I wanted to see the old camp again. As a boy I learned to take care of myself there, Konani taught me to fish in the river, the holy man taught me about plants and making medicine. I swam, ate good food, and learned of the ancestors. I met Kekoa in the old camp, and I was happy there. I wondered if Milana would also be happy.

As we walked, I sang songs, and the holy man or Milana sang with me. We ate as we walked, and did not stop, as the sun passed over our heads.

"There." The holy man pointed to the waterfall, and walked to it.

"We climb here." the holy man told Laka, and pointed to the rocks going up.

The holy man started up, and Laka followed him.

"I will take your basket." I told Milana.

She handed it to me, and began to climb up. I tied her basket to mine, and started up behind her. I looked up, saw that she took big steps with her strong legs, and used her arms also to pull herself up. Soon we stood at the top, and looked at the river.

"We will swim." the holy man told us.

I went past Laka and Milana, to the rocks by the river, and dropped the baskets and bedroll to the ground. I walked into the water, then put my arms out, and dove under. Milana was behind me, and put her head under the water.

She came up smiling, "This is good!"

Laka got into the water, and splashed it up on his body.

"Past those rocks the water runs strong, and can pull you over the waterfall." I said.

"I do not swim." he told me, "we did not have deep water near my village."

The holy man heard this, as he stepped in, "You will learn to swim." he told him.

"I like the river water." Milana said, stepped out, and lay on a rock to dry.

Laka joined her, and the holy man stood in the sun, and smiled.

"I am glad to be back."

I got out and stood by him, "I am also."

The holy man looked around, and spoke, "Laka, we will gather plants to eat."

"I will fish." I said.

"I will go with you." Milana told me.

MILANA and I stood quietly in the water. We held the ends of a net, that caught fish as they swam downstream. A fish swam into our net, we pulled it up, I grabbed it and threw it on the ground. We did this until we had enough fish to eat.

"I liked that!" she said.

"Konani taught me."

"I want to fish again." she said, and gathered the net up to carry back.

I cooked the fish over the fire, while the holy man piled plants on palm leaves. I checked the fish, and they were ready. I grabbed a palm leaf with plants, and put hot fish on top, then handed it to the holy man. I also gave this to Milana and Laka, then took mine to sit. The hot fish made the leaves warm, and soft under it. The holy man waited for me, then spoke.

"Thank you Father for a good day to travel, and thank you Mother for this fish."

He looked at Laka, grabbed plants and fish between his fingers, and ate. Laka grabbed a big bite of plants and fish, and put it in his mouth.

He chewed, then smiled, "I like this!"

"My grandmother made fish like this." Milana said, and took a big bite.

When we finished eating, I poured tea, and we sipped it as the darkness fell upon camp.

"Assistants clean after we eat." I told them, and showed them what Konani taught me.

While we cleaned, the holy man went into his hut. He came out with his feather, shell, and the plants that are tied with string. We sat down, and watched the holy man use a stick from the fire, to start the tied plants burning in his shell. He used the feather to blow the smoke around the fire pit, then walked to us, and fanned the smoke over us.

"Father and Mother we thank you for Laka and Milana," he said, "and we ask the ancestors to help teach them."

Laka's eyes did not leave the holy man. Milana looked from him to me, then back at the holy man.

"We ask the ancestors to join us." Then he sat on a log, and closed his eyes. He started to breath in and out slowly. I also closed my eyes, and breathed in deep. I slowly blew my air out, and opened my eyes. Across the fire pit, in the darkness, I saw the ancestors and said out loud, "Welcome."

The holy man opened his eyes, and looked into the darkness. "Thank you for joining us."

Laka and Milana looked into the darkness, and Laka took a quick gulp of air, as he also saw the ancestors. Milana saw them, and looked at me. I nodded.

"The ancestors are glad that Laka and Milana have joined us." the holy man said.

We sat quietly, and the ancestors went away.

The holy man stood up, "I sleep now." and he walked to his hut.

I stood up, "Come." I waved them to follow me to our hut.

I AWOKE and raised my head, to look around the hut. Sunlight was coming through the trees, and I saw Laka sleeping. I looked to where Milana slept, and her bed roll was rolled up. I smelled smoke from the fire pit, heard voices, so I jumped up and woke Laka.

"Get up." I told him, then I quickly rolled up my bedroll and left.

"How long has this camp been here?" Milana asked the holy man.

"The ancestors built it for their holy man. He did not travel, so the villagers came here to get medicines from him."

"That is hard for villages far away." Milana said.

"He taught many assistants, so they would travel around the island."

"Did many come to learn?" she asked.

"Yes, yet he would only teach those that would become healers."

"Healers?"

"A healer can hear his teacher."

The holy man smiled, and looked at me, "Does your teacher speak to you?"

I looked at him, then to Milana, "Yes." I told her.

She looked at the holy man, and squinted her eyebrows together, "Can I learn this?"

"The ancestors told me you will be a good medicine woman."

"I will hear my teacher?"

The holy man looked into the fire, "You already do."

Laka had joined us, and spoke up, "Will I learn also?"

The holy man laughed, "Yes Laka!"

I spoke up, "I will show you where the food hut is, then you and Milana will make tea, and bring food each day."

"Then we clean?" Milana asked.

The holy man told them, "You will gather fruits and fish, and prepare them. After we eat, you will clean."

I nodded to Milana, "All assistants do this."

Milana said nothing, yet she did not look happy.

"Come." I said, and walked to the food hut. I showed them baskets hanging with dried tea leaves, and other dried plants hanging. The food baskets were empty.

"We will pick fruit, and put them here." I pointed to the baskets, and we will fill this hut with many plants and medicines."

I showed them how to make the tea, and enjoyed having assistants to help.

My heart felt soft when I looked at Milana. I liked to watch her, yet when I spoke to her, I was the teacher. I wanted them to learn, and enjoy being assistants as I had. Being an assistant, is more than learning of plants. It is learning to be quiet, so that your inner teacher's voice is louder. It is being thankful for all our blessings, and giving thanks to the plants that we use. Laka and Milana must learn this, and much more.

"We will weave baskets." the holy man said.

"You will need a big basket to carry plants and fruit." I told them.

The holy man enjoyed weaving. His hut had many mats on the floor, and baskets. He made a mat that he tied to his head, and it kept the sun from his face.

"Come, we will gather what we need." he told Laka and Milana, and they followed him down the path. I grabbed my large basket, threw it on my shoulders, and walked behind them. While they gathered many kinds of plants to weave, I picked fruit and looked for plants to make medicine.

"I would like to weave a fishing net." Milana said.

"I will show you." the holy man called back.

"Milana knows how to take care of herself." I thought, "She can fight as a warrior, likes to fish, and wants to learn medicine."

I looked at her, and wondered, "Does she wants to be a mother?"

"Good." the holy man said, as he handed Laka an armful of tall reeds.

"We will split these, put water on them, to make them soft." the holy man said.

THE HOLY MAN was happy to sit in front of his hut, and weave. This was not work for him, he enjoyed it. Milana had cut long ropes that hung down from the big trees, and put them over her shoulder. The basket she carried was full of large leaves to weave.

"Are we ready?" I asked the holy man.

He looked at Laka, with both arms full of reeds, and Milana, "Yes."

We walked back to the camp, and I thought of what I would make. Just then I stepped on a rock.

"Ohh," I called out, and turned my foot over, to see a mark from the rock.

"I will make new sandals!" I said.

"I do not wear them." Milana told me.

"When we travel over hot trails around the island you will!" I told her.

"I will also make sandals." Laka said.

"Yes," the holy man said. "New sandals, and new baskets!"

We sat in camp, and the holy man showed Laka and Milana, how to weave their medicine baskets. I made new sandals, stood up, and walked around.

"These are good." I told them.

I put layers of tightly woven reeds under my feet, made straps over my toes, and another across the top of my foot.

"I like those." the holy man said.

"I will make you new sandals." I told him.

I sat down, and started to weave sandals for him. Laka and Milana worked on their large baskets, and the holy man worked on a small basket.

The day was warm, and I smelled the flowers that grew along the river. I looked over to see their colors, and saw the sun shining down on the water, as it moved toward the waterfall. The river looked so smooth, and cool, in the shade of the trees on the other side. Thinking of swimming made me smile.

"I am thankful for this day." I told them.

The holy man smiled, "This is a good day."

MANY MOONS PASSED. The holy man and I watched Milana and Laka carefully, and thought they were good assistants. They learned of plants that grew near the camp, and the holy man told them of many plants, that grew in other parts of the island. They were shown plants to hang up to dry, plants for tea, plants to use on skin, and plants to grind and mix with others. Milana was good at knowing what the medicines were for, and Laka was good at making the medicines.

The holy man was happy with them, and spent long days teaching. At night, after we ate, Laka and Milana quickly cleaned, so they could join the holy man at the fire pit. They learned of the ancestors, and how they guide us.

"Do we all have a teacher?" Laka asked.

"Yes." the holy man said.

"Why do I not hear him?"

The holy man sat quiet, looking at the fire pit.

"I do not hear them." Milana said again.

The holy man looked at her, "You have heard the voice in your head."

"My voice?" she asked.

"Your thoughts can be your teacher speaking to you."

"How do I know it is my teacher?"

"Listen, you will learn."

Laka shook his head, "Kai hears his teacher."

The holy man nodded.

Milana and Laka were quiet, looking into the fire pit.

"Listen to your thoughts carefully," I told them, "ask where they come from?"

Milana nodded.

"They can be your thoughts, your inner teacher, or your ancestor teacher."

Laka shook his head, "I do not know."

"After my medicine man ceremony," I said, "my teacher's voice is clear."

They both looked at me, and Milana asked, "The medicine man ceremony?"

The holy man spoke up, "When you are ready, I will give you the ceremony." He stood, "I sleep now."

We watched him walk to his hut, then Milana and Laka looked at me.

I whispered to them, "The ceremony will help you see, and hear your teacher."

They nodded, and were glad of this.

MILANA AND LAKA had woven large baskets for their backs, sandals, and new mats for the hut. Milana also made a small fishing net, that she used each day. They gathered the plants we ate with fish, and fruit each day. The food hut was full, and there were many medicines made.

I now knew Milana as my sister, my old thoughts of joining with her, had fallen away. I wondered how she felt, and after gathering plants, we walked back to camp.

"Will you join, and have children?" I asked.

She stopped, and made a face "Why?"

I looked at her, "You are a woman."

"I am a warrior! And I will be a medicine woman! I will not join, or have children!" she turned, and walked toward camp.

I watched her, then quickly caught up to her. She shook her head as she walked.

"I take care of myself, I do not need a man!"

I walked beside her, did not speak, and heard my teacher whisper, "She is the sister, that will be with you, when you are old."

Later, after we lay on our bedrolls, I thought of Milana. "She will be old with me." I thought, and was glad of this. I closed my eyes, and let sleep come.

"WAKE!" the holy man said, and shook my shoulder.

I opened my eyes, to see him squatting next to me. It was still dark, and I sat up.

"We must leave this day." he said.

I nodded, "I will wake them."

The holy man stood up, and walked out. I woke Laka and Milana, we walked out of the hut, and he was sipping tea.

"Good." he said, as we walked to the fire that lit our way.

"We will eat and leave." he told us.

Milana looked at me, and I shook my head.

The holy man looked at us, "I dreamed the big boat is coming."

"The big boat?" she asked.

"It brings sickness." he told her.

We ate, cleaned, and packed our baskets. The sun started to light the sky, when we walked out of the old camp, and started to climb down beside the waterfall.

"I will hold your baskets." I told Milana and Laka.

They took them off, and handed them to me. My own basket was heavy, yet I had climbed much with it.

"Watch your feet." the holy man told them, as they started to step down.

The holy man took Laka's basket from me, and I started to climb with Milana's basket over one arm. Milana and Laka jumped from the last big rock, to the dirt trail below. I quickly reached them, and handed Milana her basket.

"I could have carried it." she told me.

Behind me the holy man climbed with his, and Laka's baskets. He leaned down, handed me Laka's basket, then jumped down.

Laka took his basket, and said, "Thank you."

The holy man led us down the trail with Laka, Milana, and myself following.

"Laka said thank you, and Milana did not." I thought, "she is not happy if you help her!"

The holy man walked fast, and we traveled far before the sun was over our heads.

"We will rest." he said, and stopped.

Laka stopped behind him, and turned to look at Milana and me. His face dripped water, and he wiped it with his hand.

"I need water!" Laka said, and dropped his basket to the ground.

Milana did not drop hers, she stood, and drank from her water pouch. I took a big drink, and was glad to taste the river water from camp.

"You will get stronger." the holy man told Laka, then turned to Milana.

"You will train Laka to run on the trails."

Milana nodded.

The holy man stretched his arms around, and bent over to hang them down. I did this also, then we stood up. Milana and Laka watched.

"Do this." the holy man said, and watched them stretch, and bend down.

"We leave." he told them, and started down the trail.

THE TRAIL slowly traveled down from the high mountain camp. It wound down and out toward the sea, then turned to go back into the mountain. I watched the sun move lower to the water, and knew we would reach the village soon. The holy man came to a place on the trail where he looked down, to see the sand and village.

"Look." he said, and pointed to the water.

"A boat!" Laka cried out, "I have not seen a boat such as this!"

"I do not see Kekoa's boats." Milana said.

I stepped behind them, and looked. A boat, as tall as the trees, sat in the water. It had trees standing on it, with mats hanging down.

"Kekoa has left." the holy man said.

We stood there looking, and the holy man turned to us.

"You will not go into the village. You will hide in the mountain above the village."

"Hide!" Milana said.

"Kekoa and the warriors have left. This is the grandfather's village, and we do not know the men who traveled on this boat."

"I will protect my grandfather." Milana said.

The holy man looked into her eyes. "You will stay with Kai and Laka."

Milana looked at me, then back at the holy man. "Tell my grandfather I am here."

The holy man nodded, "I will tell him."

We walked further down the trail, then hid in the trees, on the mountain above the village.

"Stay here." the holy man said, "Kai will lead you when I am gone."

I looked at Milana, and she pulled her eyebrows together.

"I am a medicine man," I told him, "they are assistants and will follow me."

He looked at them, then he clapped me on the arm.

"Travel well." I told him.

He looked in my eyes, and I saw fear. I grabbed his arm, "What will you do?"

"The ancestors guide me." he said, "they guide you also."

When he said this, my skin got bumps, and I felt a sickness in my belly. I wanted to speak, yet I could not. We watched him walk away, and water came into my eyes. He spoke of dark clouds, and sickness coming with this boat. I knew the holy man was in danger, yet he wanted me to protect Milana and Laka. I looked at them, saw fear in Laka, and anger in Milana.

"We wait." I told them, and sat down.

CHAPTER 9

We waited. Laka and I sat leaning against trees, while Milana walked past us, then back again.

"Where is he?" she said, and stopped in front of me, "I need to know my grandfather is safe!"

"He told us to wait," I said in a strong voice, "we wait!"

She shook her head, and started to walk again. I wanted the holy man to return also, and did not know how long I could keep Milana hiding on the mountain.

"We will not have a fire." I told them when the sun dropped down.

We ate, and when darkness came, we lay out our bedrolls. Milana lay down, with her back to us.

"How long will we wait?" Laka asked.

"I do not know."

"What will we do, if he does not return?"

"Go to sleep Laka." I told him, I did not want to think of the holy man not returning.

I lay back with my hands behind my head, and looked up. The trees blocked the sky, I closed my eyes, and soon slept.

. . .

"SHE IS GONE!" Laka shook my shoulder.

I sat up quickly, and looked through the darkness to Milana's bedroll.

"When did she leave?"

"I woke, and she was gone."

"She went to the village." I said, and a bad feeling came over me.

I jumped to my feet, "Stay here with the baskets." I told him, "I will find her."

Laka looked at me with fear.

"If I do not return, you must leave, and follow the trail to my father's village."

Laka said nothing.

"Can you do this?" I asked him.

He nodded his head, "Yes."

"Take what you need from our packs, and leave."

Laka did not speak, yet his face told me, he did not want to leave.

"Do not wait for the sun, leave when darkness hides you on the trail."

Laka shook his head.

"I will find her, and we will follow you."

I bent down to grab the sharp blade from my pack, then stood, and clapped him on the arm.

"You will see us again." I told him, and walked quickly toward the village.

I DID NOT WALK on the trail, I walked quietly through the trees above the village. The moon was small, yet I knew this area well, and planned to come up behind Milana's grandfather's hut. Suddenly I heard men's voices, I stopped and listened.

They laughed, and spoke in words I did not know. I walked carefully from tree to tree, looked out, and saw men standing on the trail. They were covered in cloth, and had

large blades hanging from their waists.

"They are watching the trail," I thought, "they are warriors!"

I knew the village was in danger. I backed slowly away, and walked quietly toward the huts. Far away I saw the fire pit with a tall fire, and many men standing around. I saw Milana's grandfather's hut, and went to it. I looked around the corner for warriors, then stepped inside the hut. It was dark, yet I saw Milana and her grandfather, sitting in the corner.

"Milana." I whispered.

"Kai."

"Take her away." her grandfather told me.

I sat down beside them, "Have you seen the holy man?"

"They keep him in a hut by the fire pit." her grandfather whispered.

"Is he hurt?"

"No."

"Why do they keep him?" Milana asked.

"They think he is a chief," her grandfather said, "they will take him on the boat."

I took in a big breath and blew it out, while I tried to think on this.

"Did Kekoa leave before the boat came?"

"Yes, they left after you went to the old camp."

"What do these men want?" I asked.

"They looked in all the huts, and asked us what we trade."

"Trade?"

"The men wanted women," her grandfather said, and looked at Milana, "we said the young passed with sickness."

"The holy man said the boat would bring sickness." I told him.

"Yes, they carry sickness."

"What kind of sickness?"

"Thick water, the color of plants, comes from their noses and mouths."

"Thick water?" Milana asked.

"Such as a wound that does not heal." he said.

I had not seen sickness such as this, and wondered what medicine would help.

"We will take you with us." Milana told her grandfather.

He put his hand on her leg, "You leave, and travel fast to warn the other villages."

"We will." I told him.

"I will not leave you." Milana said.

"I am old, they will not hurt me."

"We must go" I told her.

Milana wrapped her arms around her grandfather, and lay her head on his shoulder, "Grandfather."

"I will not pass while you are gone." he told her.

She leaned back, and whispered to him, "I will return."

"Go now." he told her.

"Stay away from these men." I told him.

"I watch for the holy man." he said.

"Good." I stood up, walked to the door, and looked out.

"We must leave." I whispered.

Milana kissed her grandfather's head and stood up.

"Travel well." he told us, and we ran through the darkness into the trees.

We reached the area where Laka sat, smiling when he saw us.

"I am happy to see you!"

I told him of the holy man, then "We will travel to warn my father's village."

We put on our baskets, and I led the way. It was dark, yet I knew this trail, and walked fast. They followed, we did not speak, and traveled quickly through the night.

When we were close to my father's village, the sun started to light the trail. I thought of my brothers leaving to fish, I wanted to run, and warn them.

"I will run." I told them, and started down the trail.

"I will also." I heard Milana say.

I ran, and heard Milana behind me. I wondered if Laka ran behind her, yet did not think he could. He was not yet strong, and carried a heavy basket.

"Do not think of him." I heard my teacher say, and knew he would be safe.

. . .

RUNNING THROUGH THE HUTS, past the fire pit where my father sat, my brothers were in their boat on the water. I ran to the water, waved my arms, and yelled for them to return. They smiled and waved, then paddled back to the sand.

"Thank you Father." I leaned down with my hands on my knees, breathing hard.

"Brother!" they called, as they pulled their boat out of the water.

I stood up, and took my basket off.

"Welcome!" Jatu called, as they walked to me.

I stood there, not smiling, and wondered what we would do.

"Why are you here?" He asked when he saw my face.

"Come." I told them, and we walked to the fire pit.

Milana had told my father, and the other men at the fire pit.

"What is this?" my brother asked when he saw the men.

There was much talk, and some men wanted to fight.

"We cannot fight these warriors." I told them. "I have seen the long blades they carry."

I told them the grandfather's village said sickness made the young pass.

"As they told the chief's son." a man said.

"Where is Kekoa?" my father asked.

"He and the warriors returned to the new island, before the boat came."

"What can we do?" my brother asked.

"We will take the young to the flat lands, " I said, "they will be safe there."

"The young will travel fast," my father said, "the old will stay here."

"We must leave now." I said.

My brothers, and the other men around the fire pit, left to prepare their families. I stood beside my father, and put my hand on his shoulder.

"Drink tea." he told me.

I sat down beside him, and Milana got tea from the fire.

"Where is your other assistant?" my father asked.

"He is coming."

"There." Milana said, and pointed to Laka walking to us.

He reached us, dropped his basket, and sat down.

"Drink tea," I told him, "we leave for the flat lands."

"I need rest!" Laka cried out.

"Not this day!" Father told him.

"We will hide the boats." my brother said, as he and other men, stood on the sand by their boats.

"We will see you on the trail." I told them.

The villagers started to gather around.

"We will leave!" I told them, "get all those that will go."

Soon fathers, mothers, children, young men and women stood around with the elders.

I put my arms in the air, and closed my eyes. "Ancestors we ask you to guide us. We ask you to protect the families that travel, and the families that stay."

"Yes!" they shouted.

"Travel well!" my father said, and the grandfathers and grandmothers started saying this to their families.

"We will travel fast." I told the villagers, then led them away.

The children were happy, ran and laughed. Yet the young men and women did not smile, as they carried bed rolls, baskets and babies. I looked to see what I could carry for the others, and quickly filled my basket.

"Milana!" I called to her, and she walked away from a young mother.

"You walk behind the villagers, and watch for warriors on the trail or the water."

She nodded, "Yes."

"If you see them, hide the villagers."

Laka stood by and listened, I turned to him, "You walk with the villagers, and help them."

We walked on the sand, and I looked out to the water. I saw the men in fishing boats ahead of us. Far ahead I saw a cliff, and knew the men would hide the boats on the other side. The sun was over our heads, and the sand was getting hot. I walked closer to the water where the sand was wet, then looked behind me to see the villagers following. They had not fallen behind, and I heard them talking as we traveled.

"Good." I thought, "we will camp in the mountains this night."

We stayed on the sand, and got closer to the cliff. The water had moved away from the it, yet I knew it would soon come back, to crash where we walked.

I pointed to the cliff, "We go up." and walked to it.

I looked up for a way, and saw a small trail. The villagers joined me at the cliff.

"Laka!" I called, and he walked to me.

"You go, and help the children."

He stepped up to the small sandy trail, and I waved to the children.

"Follow him." I said.

The boys and girls climbed easily behind Laka. We watched them get to the top, then I called the mothers, "Give your babies to the men, and go."

After the mothers started climbing, I told the men to follow with the babies in their arms. Milana and I watched as all the villagers climbed, and reached the top of the cliff.

"Good," I said, "we go."

Milana ran ahead of me, and quickly reached the top. She turned, and reached her hand down to me, smiling.

"Do you need help?"

I shook my head, and smiled, "No Milana!"

From the cliff, I looked for the fishing boats on the water, yet did not see them. Milana and I now walked behind the others.

"I do not feel good leaving my grandfather, and the holy man." Milana said.

"The ancestors watch over them," I told her, "we watch over the villagers."

"Look!" a child yelled, and pointed down to the sand.

I looked down from the cliff, saw my brothers, and men from the village. The villagers ahead of me called down to them, and they waved back. We walked closer, and children started to climb down the cliff. Laka tried to stop them, yet he could not, and looked back at me.

"Let them go!" I said.

Laka followed the children down, then the mothers handed their babies to the men, and climbed down after the children, and soon we all stood on the sand. My brothers walked to me.

"We have hidden the boats." Jatu told me, and pointed down the sand where the cliff stopped.

"We lifted the boats up, and covered them with tree leaves."

I looked where they pointed, "I cannot see them."

My brother smiled, "Good."

I looked around, and yelled, "We will rest."

The women sat down, and pulled fruit from their baskets. The men and children ate, then the children ran to the water, playing and splashing in it. We sat on the sand, and my younger brother had a mouth full of fruit, with juice running down his chin. He pointed up to the cliff, where I saw Milana sitting.

"Why does she eat there?" Jatu asked.

"She watches for the warriors." I told him, and looked back at the villagers to find Laka. He was sitting with young men, eating. I finished my fruit, and stood up.

"We go." I yelled, and waved for Milana to come.

THE SUN WAS NOW low to the water, I looked down the sand, and saw where the trail started up into the mountain. I led the villagers to it, and we went into the trees as we walked up. We made camp away from the trail, and lit a small fire. Mothers laid down beside their children, and slept. I sat with the men around the fire.

"We will reach the flat lands before the sun goes down." I told them.

"What will we do if the warriors come?" a man asked.

"There are many men in the villages," I said, "we will fight."

"Good!" another said.

"I sleep." I told them, spread my bedroll out and lay down.

The men put dirt on the fire, and quietly lay down by their families.

I sat up, "Milana!" I thought. "Where is she?" I had not seen her since we made camp.

I got up, saw Laka sleeping, yet not Milana. I walked back down the trail, and soon stood on the cliff, watching the waves crash.

"Kai."

I turned, and saw Milana sitting on a rock.

"Sleep," I told her, "the warriors will not travel at night."

She stood up, and walked with me back to camp. I sat on my bed roll, and watched Milana sit down on hers. She looked at me, and I pointed to her bed roll. She smiled and pointed at mine.

THE MOUNTAIN TRAIL was washed out in places, where the stream water was fiercely pushed by storms, yet the villagers traveled well. We had not stopped since leaving camp, and soon I saw the trees open up ahead. I stopped where the mountain ended, and looked at the flat lands, stretching far down to the sea.

"It is big!" Jatu said.

"There are many villages." I told him.

I called to Milana and Laka, "Join me."

They walked to me, and looked down.

"Stay with me, you will meet Konani." I told them, "he can teach you much."

I saw Maleko's, the grandparents, and Konani's huts along the trail, and further down, the huts of the holy man's family. I felt bad to tell them of the holy man.

"We go." I called out, and led them down.

I watched Maleko's hut as we walked, saw his daughters run away from it, and down to their grandfather's hut. Then I saw men walk out to the trail, and look up at us.

"They do not know it is me." I thought.

I got close enough to yell at them, and I called, "Maleko!"

The men did not hear me. "Maleko!" I yelled, waved at them, and saw him smile.

Maleko and the grandfather waited for us, looking at the families behind me.

"Come!" I told them as I walked by, "I have much to tell you."

Maleko nodded, and walked with me. The grandfather waited for the families to pass, then he followed.

"Kai!" Konani called and waved, when he saw me, then started to walk to us.

Konani's smile made me feel good, and when he got close, I clapped him on the shoulders.

He looked at me, Maleko, and the villagers, "Why do they come?"

"Come," I said, "we will take the villagers where they can rest."

Milana stepped forward, and Konani looked at the black marks on her leg and arm.

"This is Milana," I said, "there is Laka," I pointed to him. "The new assistants."

Konani nodded, and looked back at me.

"They have learned much, yet have not had the ceremony."

"The holy man will do that." he said, and we started down the trail.

"Where is Leilani?" I asked.

"She is there." he said, and pointed to the holy man's family huts.

"Speak to me." Konani said as we walked, "I feel something bad."

My heart hurt, as I told Konani of the holy man.

He stopped, "They have him?"

"Yes."

"He was in my dream." Konani said, "he told me to prepare."

"We must gather all the villages, and tell them of the warriors on the big boat." I said.

"We will prepare for another battle." Konani said, and looked around, "Where is Kekoa?"

"He returned to the new island, before the big boat came."

Konani breathed in deep, and shook his head. "We need him for this battle."

"I am a warrior!" Milana said from behind me.

Konani stopped again, and looked at her, "You are a woman!"

"Kekoa trained her," I told him, "she is a warrior."

Konani walked again, and looked at me, "Kekoa trained her to be a warrior?"

I nodded, and he looked ahead, "She is a woman." he said quietly.

LELANI and the women watched us, as we walked past them to the fire pit.

"Welcome!" Lelani called out to me.

Konani walked to her, and spoke quietly. She looked past him to the villagers, and waved to the women.

"Come." she told them.

"Where are Aukai and Kanoa?" I asked.

"They fish." Haipo said,

"Welcome!" Mano called from a hut, then walked to us.

Konani looked around, then sat down on a log. "I need tea." he said.

Milana put down her basket, dug in it for leaves, to make tea.

"She has mountain tea." I told him.

"This is good!" he said.

We drank our tea, and watched boys run, kicking and chasing a coconut. The women cut fruit, and placed it on leaves.

"It looks like a ceremony." I told Konani.

"We will thank the ancestors for your safety, and ask them to protect the holy man."

I saw Laka with young men talking, and looked for Milana. I had not seen her since she gave us tea.

"There!" Konani said, and pointed to Aukai and Kanoa.

I looked to see, and Milana walked with them. Milana carried her fishing net and fish, the brothers carried a large fishing net full of fish.

"The girl was fishing," Kanoa said, "she told us she traveled with Kai."

"Welcome!" Aukai said.

They gave the women the fish, and looked at Milana, who also gave her fish to the women.

"Cook all the fish!" Kanoa said, as he looked around at the villagers.

"Sit." Konani said, "Kai will tell you of your brother."

The brothers shook their heads, as I spoke of the warriors from the big boat, and that they held the holy man in a hut.

"This is not good." Haipo said, "when the sun rises, we will go to the old village, and send runners to the other villages."

"We will prepare." Konani said, and I knew he thought of his dream.

CHAPTER 10

I looked across the darkness, and did not see where the night sky stopped, and the sea started. Bright lights covered the sky, the moon shined on the water, and I watched the waves roll toward me. I stood on the sand, watching and listening, my thoughts were quiet.

"You will fight." I heard the holy man's voice behind me, yet when I tried to turn, I could not. My feet were stuck in the sand, and my body would not move. I struggled to see him, trying to wrestle my body around.

"Kai!" I heard, "Kai!"

My eyes opened, I was on my bed roll, in the holy man's hut. Laka stood above me.

"You dreamed." he said.

I sat up, it was dark in the hut, yet I saw Milana looking at us.

"You were calling a name!" she said, "Who is Akamu?"

I rubbed my eyes and tried to think of the dream.

"Akamu is the holy man's name." Then I knew, "He told me to fight!"

We lay down on our bedrolls, Laka and Milana went to sleep, yet I could not. I knew that we would fight another battle, and we would fight it, without Kekoa and his warriors.

"How can we protect this island?" I thought, "we do not have blades as they have."

I lay there thinking of this, and how big their wood boat was.

"Yes!" I suddenly knew how to fight them. I sat up again, "Thank you ancestors!"

I rolled up my bed roll, grabbed tea leaves from my basket, and walked out into the night. I knew where to go, and headed up the trail to Konani's hut.

"You are here!" Konani said, when he walked out of his hut, in the sun's new light.

I sat by his fire pit. "I have made tea."

He sat down by me, and smiled, "I like this!"

We sipped our tea, and I told him of my dream.

"Fight." he said, and shook his head.

"I know what we will do." I said, and told him of the wood boat.

"Yes!" Konani shouted, "we will tell all the men to prepare for this."

Konani and I walked back to tell Haipo, Mano, Kanoa, and Aukai.

"We know how to fight them!" I said, "The men must make spears, that are wrapped in coconut husks and nut oil."

Aukai looked at me, and I spoke, "We will hide in the rocks by the water, light the spears, and throw them at the ship."

"This is good!" Kanoa said.

"We cannot let them on the island." I said.

"They have our brother."

"Your brother told us to fight"

Then Konani spoke, "I feel he will pass."

A feeling came to me, "I feel this also."

"Our brother told us to fight," Mano said, and water came into his eyes, "we will prepare."

"We will fight!" Konani said.

Kanoa and Aukai left for the old village, where they would send runners, to gather the men of other villages. I looked around at the families from my father's village, and the brother's women and children.

"I will tell the women to gather coconut husks, and nut oil." Konani said.

I nodded, "I will take Milana, Laka and men to the mountains, and cut wood for spears."

Konani looked around, "Men need to fish, so the families can eat."

I put my hand on his shoulder, "Brother," then water came into my eyes.

Milana punched me in the shoulder.

"Ouch!" I called out, and looked at her.

"We must go!" she said, and walked over to Laka and the young men he spoke with.

WE WORKED HARD, the men and women from my father's village, and others that came from villages around the flat lands. Each day we made spears, gathered wood for the fire, fished, and stopped when the sun was gone. Men watched the trails, and watched the sea from the mountain, and the cliff.

"The men are ready to fight." Haipo told me.

"Maleko will fight." Konani said.

"We cannot run fast," Maleko said, "yet we throw spears strong!"

The grandfathers that sat with Maleko spoke up, "We will fight!"

"The boys will take the women and children to hide in the mountain," Kanoa said, "the boys will protect them."

Milana looked at a boy, "I will make you a spear."

"I need a spear!" called a boy, then another, "I need a spear."

"I will make you spears," she said, "and teach you to fight!"

WHEN THE SUN rose Milana showed the boys how she made a spear, and put dark marks on it.

"The ancestors will fight with you." she said.

"The marks look like the marks on your skin." a boy said.

Milana smiled, "The marks of a warrior."

The boys looked closely at her, and made such marks on their spears. I watched her teach the boys to throw the spears at trees.

"She trains them to be warriors." my teacher whispered.

The boys watched Milana carefully, and threw their spears hard at the trees.

"They will be good warriors." I thought.

We made a pile of spears high as my body, and long as a hut. Then we made a small fire pit, ready to light next to the pile. I climbed up on the rocks, and carefully walked on them to where the waves crashed. I looked down the long sand, and out to the water. In my mind I saw the big boat come in by the rocks, yet if it did not...

"We need more spears!" I yelled, "we will make more piles along the water."

The men looked at me, they were tired from stacking the spears here.

"We prepare to fight!" I told them.

We made many piles of spears, and small fire pits, along the sand from the old village to where the holy man's brothers had their huts.

After we ate, we rested at the fire pit, and spoke of what we had done.

"I will train the men." Milana said.

I looked at her standing beside me.

"They can throw spears." I told her.

"They must sleep on the sand next to the spears, and be prepared to fight, if the warriors come in a small boat."

I knew she was a warrior, yet would the men listen to her? I stood and raised my arms, the men stopped talking to look at me.

"We know Kekoa." I said, and the men gathered spoke of him as a great warrior.

"He trained Milana to be a warrior." I said. "She trains his warriors, and she knows how to fight in battle."

The villagers now looked at this young woman, with the dark

markings. She looked small standing next to me. She stood pulled her shoulders back, yet did not speak.

"She said men must sleep by each spear pile." I looked around at the men, "if a boat comes at night, we will be ready."

The men started to speak at once, "We will do this!"

Then Milana spoke loudly, "There will be no fires, and a man will watch the water, while others sleep."

The men started to talk again, and she spoke up, "When the boat is seen, one man will run to warn us. Do not light the fires and the spears, until we see where the boat goes."

"Yes!" Jatu said, "Kekoa has taught you well."

"We will not show them we are here!" a man said, and they began to speak of who would go to each pile on the sand.

I smiled at Milana, "You have done well."

Then I put my arms up again, "We ask the ancestors to fight with us."

The villagers cried out, "Fight with us!"

I spoke again, "We ask the ancestors to protect us, and keep our families safe." Again, the villagers spoke out.

Milana raised her spear, and shouted out. Then the men shouted, and I listened to their voices loudly calling into the night. I looked for Konani, saw him with his family, and he held his arms around them. Then I looked for Laka, and saw him talking to a young woman.

"Many will not return to your father's village." my teacher said.

I watched the villagers I brought here. The women were now sisters to the women here, and the children played together each day. Also, the men fished and worked together.

"I see this." I told her.

WHEN THE SUN ROSE, men walked in from the fire pits along the water, while others stayed to fish. My brothers fished with Kanoa and Aukai, and I saw they enjoyed this. We made more spears and prepared, yet as the moon got big and small again, we wondered where the warriors were.

"We are ready, where are the warriors?" shouted a man from another flat lands village.

"Do they come by land?" Mano asked.

"No!" Aukai said, "they would not leave their boat."

I listened, and thought of this. I saw Milana with the boys, and walked to her.

"Where are they?" I asked.

She looked up at me, then to the mountain. "I will take men across the mountain, and find them."

I nodded, "Watch them, yet do not fight."

"We will return when we see them."

Milana quickly gathered men to go with her. They took their bed rolls and spears, and walked away on the trail.

"Thank you for Milana." I thought, "She is a good warrior."

I saw her stop at Konani's hut, before traveling on with the men, and soon he walked to join me. He took his large medicine basket from his back, and sat it down next to us.

"We are well prepared." he said.

"Yet I have a bad feeling." I told him.

He nodded, "I have this also."

I looked at his medicine basket. "You go to the villages?"

"I cannot wait longer."

"Go to them." I said.

"Lelani is ready to hide the children." He told me.

"Good." I said, and put my hand on his shoulder, "Travel well."

He picked up his basket, and looked at me, "I dreamed you left this island."

I shook my head, " I do not want to go."

"Yet I saw you leaving with Milana, while Laka and I waved from the sand."

"Why can I not live a quiet life?" I asked my teacher. "Why can I not join with a woman, have many children, and give medicine to the villagers such as Konani?"

No answer came, so I ran down to the water.

"I will swim until my body hurts!" I thought and ran into the waves, diving under them, before they crashed down on me. The water felt good. I swam with the waves, then out to where the water was smooth, going up and down. I turned over, floated on my back, with my arms and legs spread out. The sun light dried the water on my face, and I listened to the loud cries of the sea birds.

I closed my eyes, and suddenly saw the holy man's face. I felt fear, and knew he was warning me. I rolled over, pushed the water with my strong arms, and kicked my legs fast. I rode the waves in, reached the sand, and looked up at the mountains. Milana and the men were gone.

"They are on the mountain trail!" I thought.

"What are you telling me?" I shouted to the holy man, then I saw the women and children in the camp, and I knew.

"They must go!" I thought, and ran back to tell them.

"They must go to the mountain now!" I told the men. "We will build them huts, and bring them fish, yet they must stay away."

I saw Laka, and waved for him to come to me.

"Go with them, help carry the young."

"The young cannot travel fast," Kanoa said, "they will go now."

I watched the women gather baskets of food, and their children. Men carried their bed rolls, and soon they walked up the trail to the mountain.

"Thank you." I thought, knowing the holy man was guiding us.

AS DARKNESS FELL, the men came down from the mountain, and Laka walked with them.

"We have hidden them," he said, "they will sleep by a small waterfall and pool."

"Good."

"We built huts, and made a fire pit." Aukai said.

"The boys watch the trail," a father said, "and will protect them."

"You have guided us well." Haipo said to me.

I looked at him, "I am also guided."

I looked at Laka, "We need sleep."

He nodded, "I am ready!"

I knew he was tired from carrying a child into the mountain, and helping to build huts. He was getting stronger, yet his arms looked small. We walked into the holy man's hut, and lay down on our bed rolls. I lay there thinking of Milana, wondering where she was, and what she saw. My body was tired, yet my thoughts kept coming. Finally, I felt myself drifting away into sleep, when I heard Laka's voice.

"Mother!" he called.

I sat up, and looked at him. He was sleeping, yet he raised his arms up, "Mother!"

Then his arms dropped, and he was quiet.

"His mother is with him." I thought, "she has come to protect her son."

A feeling came over me, and I knew the battle was near. I quietly got up, and walked outside.

"I will go to the men." I thought, and walked to where the men slept on the sand. The man watching the water saw me, I raised my hand, and walked further down the sand. Each pile of spears had men sleeping, and a man watching the water. I walked past all the piles, to where the long sand ended at the mountain. The moon was big, and shined on the water. I knew if the boat came, I would see it, and I climbed up the side of the mountain. I stretched and pulled myself up, using my legs and arms to climb to a rock high above the waves. I sat down, and looked out at the sea.

"No boat." I thought, "I will sit, and enjoy watching the water."

I looked at the moon and the sky.

"Where are we?" I thought, "is the moon an island? Is the sky a sea?"

I leaned back against the rock, and closed my eyes. I listened to the waves, felt the wind on my face, and soon sleep came to me.

. . .

I AWOKE SUDDENLY, leaned forward, and heard something. The moon's light shone down, and I saw it. The mats on the big boat snapped with the wind, and pushed it through the water.

"They travel at night!"

The boat was in the rolling water out past the waves, and I saw men standing on it. My heart jumped in my chest. I turned on my stomach, slid down to a rock where I could stand, and jumped down to the sand. The boat moved fast in the water, so I began to run. I ran fast, keeping up with the boat, and looked ahead to a pile of spears and men. The men already watched the boat.

"There!" they pointed to me, as I stopped.

We stood and watched the boat pass us.

"Grab the spears!" I told them, "we must run with the boat."

I reached down, grabbed spears in my arms, and ran. The men did also, and followed. At each pile of spears, more and more men gathered spears, to run on the sand following the boat. We reached the rocks, at the other end of the long sand, and the men dropped their spears next to the big pile. No one spoke.

We watched as the big mats dropped, and heard a loud splash. The boat stopped moving. We heard another splash, and we watched quietly. Then we heard men's voices, and saw a small boat coming from behind the big boat.

"Light the fire." I told them, and watched small sparks quickly burn dried leaves and become a flame.

I grabbed spears, sticking them down into the fire. The coconut husk flamed on each spear, and I ran up on to the rocks. The other men followed with flaming spears, running to where the rocks were wet with waves. The men in the boat saw us, and yelled something. I raised my arm, pulled the spear back behind my head, and threw it hard at the small boat.

I watched my spear fall at a man's feet inside the boat, and then many other spears flew at the boat. Some hit the men, some hit inside the boat, and some in the water. Soon flames rose up in the boat, and men dove into the water, swimming back to the big boat. We stood on the rocks, watched as ropes were thrown over the side, and they climbed up.

"We go back and wait." I told the men, and we climbed off the rocks, to sit on the sand.

"We saw the fire!" Jatu said, and looked at the boat.

Aukai, Haipo, Mano, Kanoa and other men joined us. We watched the small boat burn, and sink below the waves. We sat and waited, the big boat did not leave, and the sun rose above us. We saw men on the boat watching us, and I thought they must also see, the many villages here on the flat lands.

When the sun was high over our head, the big boat raised its mats, and the winds made them move. The boat slowly moved away from us, and traveled along the island.

"They will find another place to land." I said, "we will take spears, and follow them."

We gathered many spears in our arms, and walked down the sand, following the boat. We walked quickly, then ran, yet the boat was faster and soon had gone where we could not see it.

"We will find them." I told the men.

I saw the cliff trail, and led them up. From the cliff, we saw the big boat at the end of the island, where the trail to Laka's mountain village began. We walked along the cliff, toward the boat.

"The mats are dropping!" Aukai yelled.

I knew the men would land on the island, before we could get there.

"We will stay on the cliffs, and throw our spears down." I called out. My belly felt sick, and my heart was beating hard in my chest.

"I am not a warrior!" I thought, and looked at the men around me. I saw fathers that fished.

"These are not warriors!" Yet I knew we must protect our families, and our island.

"Be with us!" I called to the ancestors.

. . .

As we ran along the cliff we watched another small boat, dropped slowly down into the water. Then men climbed down ropes to sit in the boat. We watched them paddle through the waves, get out, and pull the boat up on the sand. I stopped, and put my finger to my mouth. The men stopped, and did not speak. I waved for them to get behind trees, and we looked down at the men. They looked up, yet did not see us, then walked along the sand and looked around. A man pointed at the big boat, and others started dragging the small boat back into the water.

"They get more warriors!" I said, and knew we must fight.

I ran to the edge of the cliff, and threw a spear, hitting a man in the chest. I yelled out, and ran down the cliff. I heard the men yelling, and saw them also running down the cliff throwing spears. The warriors from the big boat ran at us with the long blades, and I knocked the blade from a man's hand, before he jumped on me. We rolled in the sand, I felt him hitting me in the side, and on the head.

Suddenly blood sprayed on me, and he fell off. I looked up to see Milana, pulling a spear from his back. I jumped up to see other men from the small boat laying on the sand, or running back into the water. The village men yelled, and chased after them, throwing spears at them as they ran into the waves. Milana and I walked to the water, and looked up at the boat. They were raising the small boat up, and men climbed on the ropes to the top.

Then I heard shouting. A man on the boat, with long hair flying around his head, stood at the edge of the big boat. He yelled, and waved his arms at us.

"Is he their chief?" I asked Milana.

"Look!" Milana cried out.

Men held a man, and brought him, to where the man yelling stood. I tried to see the man they held on each side.

"It is Akamu!" Kanoa yelled.

I raised my hand up to my face, hiding my eyes from the sun, and saw him.

"It is the holy man." I said to Milana.

The man with the long hair stopped yelling, and turned to the holy man. He looked back at us and yelled again, then I saw him raise up a long blade, and my heart jumped.

"No!" I yelled, and saw the man push the blade, down into the holy man's chest.

I gulped air, and saw them push him over the side of the boat. The holy man fell far down into the water below.

"No!" I ran into the water.

I heard men yelling from the sand, and from the big boat. I did not stop. I dove under the waves, when I came up, I saw the holy man's body going up and down on the water. I swam hard, pushing my arms down into the water and kicking fast, to reach him. Yet the water took him away from me.

I heard the mats being pulled up above the boat, and as I got closer, I heard the men yelling and throwing coconuts down at me. They hit my shoulders and head, I felt pain, yet did not stop swimming. I was close to the holy man now. His head floated, yet his body was sinking. I reached out to him, and grabbed at his hair. It slipped through my fingers, and the water took him, just out of my reach.

I took in a deep breath, and dove under the water, kicking hard to put my arms around his chest. I kicked hard again, bringing my head above water, and gulping air as I pulled the holy man up beside me. I held him tightly, not wanting him to sink under again, and felt warm water pouring out of his chest on to me. I looked at his face, saw he had passed, then water pulled at me. I kicked to stay up, yet the water was strong, and pulled me toward the waves.

"Help me!" I cried out to my teacher, as I felt the weight of the holy man's body, pulling me back under the water.

I was sinking with the holy man now, yet I would not let go. The water pushed, and pulled at me. I held my breath, then I felt hands pulling me up. My head came out of the water, I gulped for air, and saw Milana and Jatu holding me up. We went up and down with the water, moving toward the sand, and soon we were pulled to the top of a wave.

"Hold on!" she shouted.

I still held tightly to the holy man's body, and felt Milana and Jatu's hands pulled away from me. We fell with the wave, I hit the sand, and my body rolled with the force of the water. I felt sharp rocks cutting my skin.

Then my head popped up, and I saw another wave crashing down on me. I held tight to the holy man, and the water dragged me under again. The holy man's body was on top of me, as my back hit more rocks. I held my breath, and pushed to move him. I came up, gulped air, and tried to get my feet under me. Another wave knocked me down, the holy man slipped from my hands, and I was dragged under water.

I felt sand under my back now, and my head and chest came out of the water. I sat up, and saw the holy man floating close to me. Milana and Jatu ran to me, and helped me stand. I watched Haipo and Kanoa pull the holy man out of the water, and as I started to walk, my legs would not carry me and I fell. Milana grabbed me, I heard her speak, yet saw only darkness. Then I heard no more.

I AWOKE ON THE SAND. It was dark, and a fire burned close by. The men stood around talking of the day, and of the holy man. I tried to get up, yet my arm would not hold me, and I fell back down.

"You live." I heard Milana say.

She kneeled beside me, and held my head up to sip tea.

I sipped the tea, and it hurt my throat. "Thank you." I whispered.

She gently laid my head down. "I will bring you fish." she said, and walked away.

I rolled to my side, and looked out to the water. The big boat was gone. Then I looked to the sand by the fire pit, and saw the holy man's body lying on palm leaves.

Water came into my eyes, and I shook my head, "No, no, no."

My heart hurt, I wiped water from my eyes, and could not believe I was seeing the holy man's body without life. He was gone, as mother had left me. I put my arm over my eyes and let the water come, it ran from my eyes, and I bit my lip to stop from crying out.

I heard someone walking to me, and put my hand up to wave them away. I lay there feeling the wounds on my body, feeling my heart hurting inside my chest, and knew the holy man did not feel this. I let myself drift away, so I would also not feel the hurt.

"I WILL FEED YOU SMALL BITES." Milana said, and lifted my head to put hot fish to my lips. I chewed and swallowed, then the fish would not stay in my belly. Milana held my hair back, as the fish came up suddenly.

"You swallowed much sea water." she told me.

"I feel sick." I said in a small voice.

"Rest." she said, and rubbed her hand across my face.

I nodded, and fell back down. My eyes closed, and again sleep came to me.

A HAND SHOOK MY SHOULDER, and I opened my eyes. I saw Milana and Jatu above me, and the sun lit the sky. My head hurt, and I had pain in my back. I pushed with my arms to sit up, they hurt and shook, as I sat up. I wanted to speak, yet no words came.

"Drink tea." Milana said, and handed me a shell.

I saw tea leaves floating on the hot water, and I sipped. She walked away, and came back with fruit.

"When did you return?"

"We came through the mountain, through Laka's village, and then saw the big boat."

Milana smiled, "We were in the trees, when I saw you throw a spear, and run down the cliff."

I thought of this, and shook my head.

"You are a good fighter, " she said, and put her hand on my shoulder, "yet I am glad I was there to help."

Jatu laughed, "We are glad you returned to fight!"

"I am glad you helped me." I told her, "are we ready to leave?"

"We have waited for you to travel." she said.

Milana gave me her hand, and I slowly stood up. I looked down at my body, it had many cuts from the rocks under the water.

"I look like a great warrior!" I said.

They looked at me, and laughed.

"Other men have wounds from battle," Jatu said, "yet not bad like yours!"

Kanoa walked to us.

"Can you travel?" He asked.

"I will walk slow." I told him.

He and Jatu walked to the men, Haipo and Mano began to pull the holy man's body on woven palm leaves, slowly down the sand. My heart hurt when I saw this, and water came into my eyes. I started to walk, and Milana grabbed my arm.

"I go to my grandfather." she said.

I looked at her, "Can you wait?"

"I saw my grandfather when I traveled across the island," she told me, "He is sick."

I looked into her eyes and saw fear, like I saw in the holy man's eyes.

"He tried to hide it," she said, "I saw him spit on the sand."

"The sickness from the men on the boat?" I asked, thinking of what her grandfather had told us.

"Yes," she nodded, "it was the color of plants."

"I will go with you." I told her, and yelled at the men.

They stopped, and Jatu walked back to us.

"Tell Konani we go to her grandfather." I told them, "He is sick, and I will give him medicine."

He nodded, "Travel well."

I watched him walk back, while others walked ahead. I looked at Milana, nodded, and we turned to walk up the mountain trail.

I THOUGHT of the holy man, who had been my father after I left my village. He had taught me much, and I thought of him as we walked. I thought how he had been young and strong. How he and Konani helped me travel to the medicine man camp, where he took me to gather plants, and showed me how to make medicine. Then I thought of the medicine man ceremony he gave me.

"Who will give Milana and Laka their ceremony?" I asked my teacher.

"You and Konani." she said.

I walked on, knowing he now lived with the ancestors, yet I wanted to see him smile, and hear him speak.

Milana stopped, and waited for me, "Do you need rest?"

I walked slowly to her, and stopped. "I need medicine."

"Tea for pain?" she asked.

I nodded, and found a tree to sit under.

CHAPTER 11

We traveled up through the mountain, and came to Laka's village.

"I must tell Laka's grandfather that he is happy." I said, and looked for him at the fire pit.

He sat with other old men, when he saw me his eyes got big, and he stood. The men walked quickly to me, looking at my wounds, and seeing my pain.

"There was a battle?" he asked, "does Laka live?"

"He did not fight, he is safe."

His grandfather took in much air and blew it out, "Good."

I smiled at him, "He is a good assistant."

His grandfather nodded, he told his friends, "My grandson learns to make medicine."

"He is happy and has many friends."

Laka's grandfather smiled, "It was good his mother made him leave."

"She watches over him." I said, "Is there a basket I can have for medicine? We must see a sick man." I told him.

"Yes! Follow me" he said, and we walked behind him to his hut.

"Laka's mother made this." and gave me a basket with a handle.

"This is good." I said, "I will give it to Laka when I see him."

The grandfather nodded, "Tell Laka to travel this way."

"I will tell him, and I will tell him you are well."

"Thank you." his grandfather said.

Milana and I waved to the men, walked through the village, and down the trail into the thick trees and plants. The trail was small, and I followed Milana. There was no wind that blew to cool us, and the air was heavy and hot. My body poured out water, and my cuts hurt. I thought of the river at the old medicine man's camp, and I heard the stream which ran close to the trail.

"I want to wash my body." I told Milana, and walked toward the stream.

It was a small stream, yet the water ran over many rocks, and it was clear.

I looked at Milana, "I will travel faster after this."

I sat the basket down next to the stream, stepped out on the rocks, and let the water run over my feet. It felt cool. Then I sat down, stretching my legs out in front of me. She dropped her spear, stepped into the water beside me, and sat down.

"This is good!" she said, and lay on her back. The water ran from the top of her head, down over her body. Her long hair went on either side of her, and she splashed water on to her face. I carefully leaned back, and felt pain when I lay down.

"Ohh" I said, and let the water run over me.

I looked up. A small bird sat on a branch over the stream, and sang. I began to sing back, which made Milana laugh.

"You sing to the birds!" she said, "I will call you mele manu." and she laughed.

I did not want to leave the cool water, and the bird that sang for us, yet I wanted to see her grandfather. I stood up, used my hands to squeeze the water from my hair, then I tied it back with a string. Milana got out of the water, and wove her hair down her back.

I grabbed the basket, and led her back to the trail. My body felt better after the water washed away the sea and sand, and I began to sing again as I walked.

From behind, I heard Milana call out "Mele manu."

BEFORE WE LEFT THE MOUNTAINS, we picked leaves for tea and medicine. I thought of the sickness that her grandfather had, and wondered what I could give him.

"Tell me what medicine I will give to him." I asked my teacher, yet no answer came.

We stood where the trail left the mountain, and looked down at the water.

"We will sleep at my father's village, and travel when the sun rises." I told her.

We walked along the sand, and spoke no more. I thought of the battle I fought, and of the holy man. My heart hurt, and my eyes filled with water again.

"Stop this!" I told myself, "he has not left you."

"Your heart will heal." my teacher whispered.

"My heart healed after mother passed," I said, "I will be glad when it heals again."

I looked ahead, and knew we would soon see my father's village. We walked around big rocks, and ahead was the fire pit, with huts behind that.

"We will eat and rest." I told Milana.

I was tired, my body hurt, and I was ready to sit. I looked to see my father at the fire pit, yet he was not there. Many others that sat around the fire pit were also not here.

"I will find my father." I said.

"I will wait." Milana said, and sat down on a log by the fire pit.

I walked to his hut, and stood at the door. My father lay on his mat.

"Are you sick?" I asked, and walked to see him.

He lay, with his eyes closed.

"Father." I said, and put my hand on his shoulder. It was hot, then he started to choke.

I rolled him on his side, and he choked more before spitting out thick water.

"The sickness from the big boat." I said, "Did the boat come here?"

My father nodded, "They took us to the fire pit."

He opened his eyes, and looked at me.

"They slept in our huts, with young women they took from other islands."

I put my hand on his forehead, and it was hot. "You need medicine."

He grabbed my hand, held it, and looked into my eyes.

"The women were sick also, and the men beat them."

He closed his eyes, and shook his head slowly from side to side. I saw water roll down his face.

"I heard them scream and cry," he said, "yet I could not help."

"Where did you sleep?" I asked.

He opened his eyes, yet still held my hand.

"On the sand by the fire pit."

"I will get you medicine." I said, and took my hand from his.

"It is good you took our families to the flat lands." he told me, and closed his eyes.

I watched him, his chest breathed hard, and water rattled in his throat.

"I will get water from the river," I thought, "and cool him."

I walked back to the fire pit, and stood by Milana.

"My father is sick also."

She looked at me, "I must go to my grandfather!" She stood up, and grabbed the basket full of plants, and tea leaves."

"Darkness comes." I told her, yet I knew she would travel in the darkness.

"I will go." she said, "take what you need." and she handed me the basket.

I grabbed plants and tore leaves from them, then gave it back.

"I will join you." I told her.

Milana put her hand on my shoulder, opened her mouth to speak, then stopped.

"Go." I said, she turned, and ran through the huts to the mountain trail.

I knew that Milana would travel through the night, to be with her grandfather.

"Let her grandfather not pass, until she is with him." I asked the ancestors.

WHEN I RETURNED to father's hut with the cool water, he slept on his side. His breathing was loud, and he choked with the thick water, that filled his mouth. I pounded his back with my hand, and he spit it out. His body was hot, and I poured the water over his head, yet he did not wake.

"Will father pass also?" I thought, then through the darkness of the hut, I saw mother.

I was glad to see mother, yet my heart, hurt knowing she was here to guide father. I shook his shoulder, and heard his chest full of water when he breathed.

I let go, and dropped my head. Water fell from my eyes, and my shoulders shook. The holy man had passed, now father. I looked back at mother, and she nodded.

"It is his time." I heard my teacher say, yet I was not ready. I lay down beside father, and listened to him breath, many times I pounded his back, so he would spit the thick water out. Then my body, hurting and tired from wounds, called me to sleep.

FATHER WENT with mother that night, and many other grandfathers and grandmothers from the village, also passed to live with the ancestors. The sickness brought from the big boat killed the old, as the blade had killed the holy man.

We did not take their bodies to the caves, there were more than we could carry. We wrapped them in palm leaves, and lay them by the water, where grandmothers poured nut oil on them, and made a fire. When the bodies were burned, the ashes were swept down into the water, and we watched it taken away into the sea. The elders that did not pass, stood around me.

"We will go to the flat lands." a grandmother told me, "we will join our families there."

"I cannot take you now." I said, "I must go to another village."

She smiled, "I am old, yet I traveled this island when I was young."

Another grandmother spoke up, "We will go."

A grandfather held his hand up, "I will take you." and other old men said they would help.

I watched them speak of preparing to leave. They did not want to stay in this village, they spoke of the sickness, and the big boat.

"I will not stay for it to return!" a woman said.

I looked around at the village, and thought of growing here, with my family. Now no families would be here, the huts would be empty.

"Your families will be happy that you join them." I told them.

We ate around the fire pit, and I listened to the grandfathers and grandmothers speak of those that had passed. I stood up, and raised my arms to the sky. The elders got quiet.

"We know that you are with us," I said, "you guide us now."

I heard an old man call out "Yes!"

"Take them to their families," I said, "protect them."

The grandfathers and grandmothers yelled out, "Protect us!"

I walked away from them, and walked on the sand by the water. I sat, looked at the water, and listened to the small waves rolling in.

"Thank you father," I spoke out loud, "thank you Akamu."

"I am glad you were with me," I felt water in my eyes, "and taught me well."

I took in a big breath, and blew it out. My body hurt, and my eyes were tired. I lay down on my side, and watched the water until sleep came.

Sun came into my eyes, and I sat up. I brushed sand from my face, and arm, then stood.

My belly was hungry, so I walked back to the fire pit.

"Milana!" I called out.

She sat, with her back to me, looking at the fire. I walked behind her, and put a hand on her shoulder. She jumped, and turned to look at me.

I saw her face and knew, yet I asked. "Did your grandfather pass?"

She nodded, and looked back at the fire.

"My father also." I told her, and sat down.

Milana looked up at me, "They all passed." she said, "I made medicines..." she stopped and swallowed.

"Our medicines cannot fight this sickness." I told her.

"I put them together in a big hut, and covered them with flowers."

She looked into the fire, "I closed the hut with logs and lit a fire."

I put my hand on her shoulder.

She sat up straight, "Grandfather waited for me to pass," she said, "he smiled and held my hand."

I nodded, and thought, "Thank you ancestors."

"The village is empty?" I asked.

"Yes," she looked around, "not all passed here."

"No, we will take them to join their families on the flat lands."

She nodded, "Good."

I grabbed a large log, and threw it on the fire.

"I want to return to the new village." she told me.

I watched the wood start to burn, and thought of what she said.

"Help me build a fast boat." She said.

I looked at her, thought of Konani's dream, and knew I would leave the island with her.

"I will help build it," I told her, "and I will go with you to join Kekoa."

CHAPTER 12

Milana and I traveled back to the flat lands, with the grandmothers and grandfathers. The elders walked slow, yet they did not stop. They picked fruit as we traveled, spoke of those that had passed, and enjoyed looking at the island. Milana and I gathered plants for medicines, and the grandmothers wanted to learn of this. When Milana spoke of traveling on the long boat, the grandfathers told Milana they would help build it.

"I will help build your new huts." I told them.

I was happy they wanted to live on the flat lands, they would be safe if the big boat returned.

"There." I pointed to the flat lands, and the many huts spread across it.

The grandmothers and grandfathers were happy to be here, they wanted to see their families. When we walked out of the mountain, and down the trail, my heart hurt. I would have to tell my brothers of father passing, and I wondered what Konani would say of the holy man. He had been gone when the big boat came, he did not see the battle, yet he saw the holy man's body pulled home.

I saw Maleko sitting in front of his hut. He got up, and waved as he walked. I saw that he looked old, and walked with stiff legs.

"Welcome!" he yelled.

"Maleko!" I yelled back, and waved, yet we did not stop.

We came to the grandfather's huts, then Konani's, and Leilani waved to us.

"Konani?" I called out.

"He travels to the other villages." she said.

We walked by, and got closer to the huts around the fire pit, where the holy man's brothers lived. Aukai and Kanoa stood by the fire pit, with my brothers, after fishing this day. They watched us walk into camp.

"Welcome!" they called out.

Milana spoke up, "We have brought the elders that did not pass with sickness."

FAMILIES from the village walked close, and asked of their fathers and mothers. Women cried out, and water rolled down their faces, when they learned of their passing.

Jatu came to me, "Father?"

I looked into his eyes, "He passed to be with mother."

He shook his head, "No! He is gone!"

I put my hands on his shoulders, "He watches over us."

Kanoa looked at the elders, "We will build many new huts."

"And a fishing boat." Aukai said.

"We also need a fast boat to travel to Kekoa." I said, and looked at Milana.

"You will leave?" Jatu asked Milana.

"I will train the young men to be warriors, and guard the island from all sides." Milana said, "Then I will leave."

"It is good that our families are prepared." Haipo said.

"Where is Laka?" I asked.

"He went with Konani to the villages."

We stood around the fire pit, and I learned of the ceremony given for the holy man.

"We had a great feast." Kanoa said, "many came from the other villages."

The women brought fruit, and cooked fish on the fire. I saw that many huts had been built around Kanoa, Haipo, Mano and Aukai's huts. Now more would be built, and this would be a new village.

I raised my arms. "Great Father and Great Mother, we thank you for this island, and for the sea."

I looked around at the children, men, women and elders, "Ancestors we thank you for guiding us, and protecting us."

I had not seen Konani and Laka walk behind me, and I heard Konani's voice, "We thank our ancestors, for bringing Kai and Milana back safely."

I turned to see his face. Water came into my eyes, I took a step to him, and grabbed his shoulders.

"Konani!"

THERE WAS much talk around the fire. I told my brothers of father's sickness, Laka listened to Milana talk of the battle, and Konani spoke of the ceremony for the holy man's passing.

"He is up there." he pointed to the mountain, "looking down on us. We made a big pile of rocks, and put flowers in the dirt, to grow around him."

"I want to see this." I said.

"You have many wounds." Konani said, and looked at my arms and legs. "I was told you swam for the holy man's body."

"I swam," I said, and smiled, "Milana had to pull me out of the water."

He looked into my eyes, "Thank you Kai."

I felt water in my eyes again, and looked away at Laka. "Does he make a good medicine man?"

"He knows many medicines now."

"Will you give him the ceremony?"

"When he is ready." Konani answered, "how is Milana?"

"She has been a warrior. She needs to learn more medicine, then I will give her the ceremony."

The fish was cooked, and many fruits and green leaves were passed around. Konani joined Leilani and their children to eat, and Laka walked over to the same young woman, that he spoke with before the battle. I saw the women helping each other, children playing, and men talking around the fire pit.

"This will be a great village." I thought.

I looked for Milana, saw her speaking with young men, and knew she prepared them to be warriors.

When she returned with Kekoa to the grandfather' village, I thought I wanted to join with her, now I did not feel this. Before the battle, and the sickness that took many, I enjoyed traveling the island as a medicine man, yet now I was ready to leave. I would travel with Milana to a new island, and I wondered if the ancestors would bring me back to see Konani and my family, or send me down a new path.

"Will I return to live here?" I asked my teacher.

"Your heart will guide you." she answered.

THE ELDERS WERE happy to sit outside their new huts, weaving mats and baskets, and watching the children play. The women worked as sisters, caring for their children, and they smiled much. My brothers fished in their new boat, with the other men, and Milana's boat was being built by the villagers.

While the boat was being built, she took young men down the sand to the end of the island. She told them to build piles of spears, a small fire pit, and that they must live here watching for the big boat.

Milana told them that when the moon was big, they would come back to the village, and others would go to live there. Then she took more young men across the mountain, to the other side of the island, and told them to do the same. She spoke to them of what Kekoa taught her, trained them, and told them to train others to be warriors after she was gone. The new warriors were happy to do this.

. . .

MILANA RETURNED from the other side of the island, and she joined me at the fire pit.

"A young man asked me," she said, "must we live away from the village until the big moon?"

I smiled, "What did you say?"

"Kekoa taught me that a warrior must learn to live without a hut, and without his family."

"Medicine men also do this." I said.

"I told them to make a hut, fish, and train together."

"They will get stronger." I said.

"I told them to run on the sand, and swim in the waves."

"Kekoa will be happy with you."

"I wanted to be a medicine woman, yet I am happy to train these young men."

"You have learned to make many medicines," I said, "and these will help your warriors."

Her eyes got big, "I will not give medicines to the villagers, I will give it to the warriors!"

"The ancestors have guided you!" I told her.

"How have they guided you?" she asked.

"I am guided to do what is needed," I said, and looked out to the sea.

"Does this make you happy?"

I looked back at her and smiled, "I am thankful for my blessings."

"Do your blessings make you happy?"

I thought on this, "I have what I need, I do not want more."

Milana punched me in the arm, "You do not answer me!"

I laughed, "I am happy when you do not hit me!"

Milana laughed now, and rubbed my arm, "I did not know that I could make you happy!"

. . .

THE MEN of the village waited for Milana to wake, and when she walked out of the holy man's hut, they called out, "Milana!"

She asked, "What is this?"

The men took her arms, and walked her to the water. I followed, and looked over their heads to see what was ahead. I saw the boat was finished. It was wide and long, so that many men could travel in it. The boat and paddles were made from strong wood that grows on the mountain. The paddles were also long, and would reach wide and push the boat quickly through the water.

Milana saw it and smiled. She put her hand on the boat, and walked around it, still touching the wood. She picked up a paddle, held it up, and looked down the straight shaft.

"You have built a good boat, she said and smiled, "Kekoa will be pleased."

She stepped into the boat and sat down, "I am happy!"

The men were glad that she liked the boat, and told her of gathering the strongest wood from the mountain. We looked over the boat, then walked back to the fire pit. We drank tea and ate fruit.

"We will prepare to leave." she told me.

I HELPED Konani and Laka make many medicines, then Konani and I rested at the fire pit after eating, and watched Laka again, sitting next to the same young woman. Konani sat next to me.

"They will join." he told me.

I looked at them, "They are young to join."

Konani laughed, "Are you looking with old eyes my brother?"

I laughed, "To my old eyes they look young!" I said, then "what of your daughters?"

Konani pulled his head back, "My daughters are still young!"

"Are there young men talking to them?" I asked.

He shook his head, "They are not ready."

I laughed, Konani pushed me and spoke, "Do not speak of this!"

"I will travel to see that the warriors are guarding the island." Milana told me.

I knew she would want to leave when she returned.

"I will see that they have made spears, and fire pits, and tell them that a man must watch through the night, as the others sleep."

She stopped, and looked at me, "They must be strong."

I nodded, "Tell them to swim each day,"

"They must run, and train to fight also." she said.

Milana left when the sun rose, and took young warriors she trained, to travel with her around the island.

I swam each day, and ran on the sand. I wanted to be strong to travel, and I was. My arms and legs had grown larger, and my belly was flat. Many young women served me food and smiled, yet I thought of them as sisters. Only Milana had made me think to join with her, and now I felt that she was also my sister.

The night had come, Konani left with his family to sleep in their hut, and I watched Laka speak to the young woman that he would join with.

"Will I join with a woman?" I thought, yet no answer came.

I walked into the holy man's hut, and lay down on my bed roll. I looked around. The holy man was gone, Konani was gone, Laka and Milana were gone, and the hut was dark and quiet.

I closed my eyes, and suddenly I saw a face. She was smiling. Her hair was dark, with light strands weaving through it. Her eyes were dark, and her skin was light like my mothers.

Her face went away, and I looked through her eyes at the sea. She felt at peace, looking over the water, and I felt this also. She was happy, laughed much and I knew that she waited for me. Then she was gone, and I fell asleep thinking of her.

When I awoke I still felt her, I knew what was in her heart.

"I will join with her." I thought, and knew she would be a good woman for me.

"Thank you." I told my teacher.

I have not met her, yet now I know she waits for me.

. . .

MILANA RETURNED from the other side of the island, and walked to me.

"The men are ready. I found a man sitting by the fire watching the water, as the others slept."

"Good" I said.

"We must prepare to go." she told me.

I nodded, "What will we need to travel?"

"Dried fish, fruit, water, and fishing mats."

"Fishing mats?" I asked.

"Yes, we will take those also, for the water that comes down."

I thought of being on the water, and the water coming down on us. "How long will we travel?"

"Many suns." she said, and walked to our hut.

I looked out to the sea, and did not want to go.

"How will we find the new island and Kekoa's village?" I thought, yet Milana said she knew this.

"Ancestors travel with us, and protect us." I said, knowing the ancestors would guide me.

MILANA CHOSE the young warriors that would travel in the boat with us, then we walked down to the sand.

"We will run, and push the boat into the water." she said, "and paddle quickly straight into the waves."

We did as she told us, and as we paddled toward a wave, I wondered if it would break on us, and push us over.

"Paddle!" she yelled.

We pulled our paddles back together, and the boat pushed forward in the water. A wave rose higher in front of us, the boat rose up and we paddled hard, to push through it before it crashed down. Suddenly the front of the boat dropped down, and I looked ahead, to see another wave coming.

"Paddle!" she yelled again.

My heart pounded in my chest, and I thought of rolling under the waves along the rocks. Again, we pulled back the paddles, again the boat pushed forward, and we went up and over the wave. I saw the water ahead rolling in toward us, and was glad we had passed through the waves.

"Paddle!" Milana yelled.

We took the boat out to smoother water. The boat moved fast after we were past the waves, and we paddled together.

"Good!" Milana yelled, "now we turn!" and she pointed to go along the island.

We traveled far, following the island, and I felt the sun on my shoulders. Milana told us to ride the waves in to the sand, then we jumped from the boat, and pulled it out of the water.

"This is a good boat!" she yelled out.

She looked at me, then at the others, "Put mud on your bodies, the sun will not burn your skin."

We ate dried fish, and drank water that she brought in the boat.

"We will travel under the sun, and the moon. Some will sleep while others paddle, and we will not stop." she told us.

"How will we find the island?" a young man asked.

"We travel this way" she pointed to the end of our island, "then follow the sea birds when they fly under the sun, and follow the night lights that Kekoa showed me, under the moon."

I wondered about this, "When will we see the island?"

"We must travel far, then you will see it, and travel more to get there."

"We go back." Milana told us, and we took the boat back into the water.

WE HAD LEARNED how to paddle through the waves, and quickly through the smooth water. We took the boat out into the water much to prepare. The young warriors and I felt good about paddling, and traveling fast.

Winds were bringing in dark water clouds, and I did not think we would go out this day.

"Come!" Milana said, "we will paddle in the rough water."

We took the boat out, and after we paddled through the waves, the water took us up and down with waves the sea brought from far away.

"This is good!" she yelled, "this helps us prepare."

We paddled long on these waves, and when the dark clouds poured water on us, we pulled the fishing mats over our heads and still paddled. When the sun dropped down close to the water, we pulled the boat on to the sand, and my arms and back hurt from paddling. The young warriors were tired also, and soon after we ate, we left to sleep in our huts.

I lay on my bedroll, drifting into darkness, when I heard Milana's voice.

"Mele manu" she said, "we are ready to leave now."

I did not answer, and let myself fall into sleep.

THE SUN ROSE, and the dark clouds were gone. I saw them far away over the mountains, as I walked out of the hut. Milana had already made tea, and was happy to speak of leaving.

"We will gather our food and water" she said, "and pack the boat with the nets and mats"

I nodded and sipped my tea.

"We will take tea leaves to chew." she said.

I looked at her, "Tea leaves?"

"Kekoa made us chew tea leaves to stay awake, and paddle in the darkness."

"The holy man gave Konani and I tea leaves to chew, when we traveled."

"We will leave when the sun rises." she told me.

She gave me a piece of fruit, and looked around. "Where is Laka?"

"I have not seen him."

Milana and I sat sipping our tea, when Laka joined us.

"Laka!" I said, "where have you slept?"

He smiled, and pushed back his hair from his face. "In my woman's hut."

"Your woman?" I asked.

"We have not joined, yet her father asked me to stay in their hut."

"He said you can join with her?" Milana asked.

Laka nodded, "Yes." he said, "I must build a hut before we join."

"I am happy." I told him, "yet we will travel when the sun rises, and I cannot help you."

"Konani will help," Laka said, "and my woman's brothers."

"Your new brothers." I told him.

He smiled, "My brothers."

I knew he was happy to have a family, yet his grandfather still lived in the mountain village.

"You must travel to your grandfather, and ask if he will be at your joining."

"I have thought of this," Laka said, "and I will also ask him to live here with me."

"This is good." I was happy that his grandfather would be in this village, with the other elders.

THE MEN FISHED, and the women prepared it, and fruit for a feast. Milana, the young men and I packed the boat, and many villagers came to see us at the fire pit.

"Travel well." they told us, and clapped us on the arms.

Jatu sat with me, "We will build a hut for you."

"Thank you." I told him.

"You will return?" Konani asked me.

I looked at my old friend. "I want to yet I do not know."

Konani nodded, "The ancestors will guide you."

Yet as I looked into his eyes, I saw he was sad, and wondered if he knew I would not return.

Milana looked at the sky, "There are no clouds."

"This is good." Jatu said.

Konani stood, raised his arms, and we stopped talking.

"Ancestors!" he yelled, "travel with Kai, Milana and these men."

The villagers nodded.

"Take them to Kekoa safely." he said.

I looked around, and saw the fathers and mothers of the young men were sad.

"The ancestors will protect us!" I yelled, "The young men will return to their families!"

"Yes!" they cried out.

The women passed the fish and fruit around, and we ate. Maleko joined Konani and me.

"Drink this." he said, and gave us a coconut.

I put it to my mouth, and when I drank, it burned my throat. I coughed and made a face.

Maleko laughed loudly, "This was given to Konani when he joined with my daughter."

"It was!" Konani said, and laughed.

My brothers also drank from the coconut. Soon we laughed, and my body felt warm. I looked around at villagers enjoying the feast.

"These are my family." I thought, "this is my village."

I wrapped my arms around my brothers.

"Travel well." Jatu told me.

Then I turned to look at Konani, we stepped to each other, and wrapped our arms around each other.

Konani whispered in my ear, "You are my brother. I will see you again, here or in the village of our ancestors."

I stepped back from him, and saw water in his eyes. I also had water in my eyes, and I nodded. "We are brothers."

ABOUT THE AUTHOR

APRIL AUTRY

April writes about her spiritual journey, including many of her past lives.

    April is an Intuitive mentor, Quantum healer, Reiki master, Yoga teacher, and teaches alignment of your mind-body-soul through consciousness expansion and spiritual practices. Books, blog, shop and services can be found on her website:

> https://GalacticGrandmother.com

    April enjoys reading your book reviews, so please feel free to email her at:

> https://info@galacticgrandmother.com

www.ingramcontent.com/pod-product-compliance
Lightning Source LLC
LaVergne TN
LVHW051559080426
835510LV00020B/3051